Aviation and Hospitality

Aviation and Hospitality

Shailendra Sengar

ANMOL PUBLICATIONS PVT. LTD.
NEW DELHI-110 002 (INDIA)

ANMOL PUBLICATIONS PVT. LTD.
H.O.: 4374/4B, Ansari Road, Darya Ganj,
New Delhi-110 002 (India)
Ph.: 23278000, 23261597

B.O.: No. 1015, Ist Main Road, BSK IIIrd Stage
IIIrd Phase, IIIrd Block
Bangalore - 560 085 (India)
Visit us at: www.anmolpublications.com

Aviation and Hospitality

First Published, 2008

ISBN 978-81-261-3439-7

PRINTED IN INDIA

Printed at Mehra Offset Press, Delhi.

Contents

Preface

This Encyclopaedic Series of Career and Vocational Guidance Covers careers, describing jobs, places of employment, working conditions, qualifications, education and training. This has been developed to aid career and counsellors and job placement coordinators in planning activities for students and potential students about career vocational education programs. It contains a career and vocational guidance model which clarifies what career and vocational guidance services mean and what planners should include in their activities. The model shows an interrelatedness among major thrusts with career development being a central theme of vocational guidance. All of the thrusts depicted in the model represent essential services that should be available to students in career and vocational education programs. The encyclopaedia deals with various sections which correspond to the major thrusts identified in the model: (1) career development; (2) recruitment; (3) guidance and counselling; (4) placement; (5) follow-up and follow-through; and (6) consultation. Each section contains an outline of the perceived needs of the topic, an overview of the topic relative to career and vocational guidance, and some suggested activities and strategies that may be useful in meeting student needs.

It also contains current information about occupations, employment trends, and job searching. Materials on career decision-making, internships, and salaries are also located in each volume. This Series of Encyclopaedia helps students assess their potential for various careers.

Shailendra Sengar

1

Introduction

Hospitality

The Hospitality industry consists of the hotels/lodgings and restaurant/food service sectors. If enjoy meeting lots of different people or working in an environment that is as different every day as the people coming through your establishment, you should consider these two sectors.

People in the hotel and lodging sector make sure that guest accommodations are pleasant, comfortable and that everything in the hotel runs smoothly. The range of opportunities and the locations of workplaces are enormous. In the US alone, there are over 60,000 establishments from the small boutique hotels to the internationally famous resorts.

In the restaurant and food service sector you can go from an entry-level position like prep chef to running your own kitchen as an executive chef at a five star establishment! This sector is one of the nation's largest employers. Many young adults start their work lives in this sector but with a little hard work and/or additional education, a rewarding career path is also available.

The diverse range of activities offered by this industry provides excellent job opportunities for people with varied skills and educational backgrounds. Jobs will be plentiful for first-time job seekers, senior citizens and those seeking part-time or alternative work schedules.

Training for food service managers is available through industry-sponsored seminars; short-term, subject-specific certificate programmes; or Associate and Bachelor's degree programmes in management.

A certification in hospitality management can be obtained through an 18-month training course or a 4-year specialized Bachelor's degree.

The Hospitality industry is growing rapidly, which means there are many great career opportunities in the years ahead!

Careers in Hospitality

For many people the thought of a career in hospitality, leisure and tourism brings up images of chefs, fitness instructors and overseas reps....and nothing else! Well of course, these are all careers that fall within these sectors, but there is so much more to consider....in fact much, much more, the hospitality industry alone employs 1 in every 10 people in the UK, that's over 2.5 million people working in more than 30,000 establishments. Also, 1 in every 5 new jobs fall into this sector with another 400,000 new jobs created by 2006 according to The British Hospitality Association. That's a lot of jobs!

Not just chefs and waiters then? No way... this is a huge industry offering variety, diversity and tons of different jobs and career opportunities to suit everyone.

So what sort of person do you need to be to work in hospitality, leisure and tourism. Well to begin with you need to like people and enjoy the challenge of working in a customer focused environment. You need to be flexible, adaptable, enjoy problem-solving and thinking on your feet and to be able to work as part of a team.

Michelle Davies is 21 and is a Receptionist with hotel group Jarvis. Michelle says that the diversity of the industry brings challenges and new opportunities and that's what appeals to her. She says, "I originally came to Jarvis when I was on a year's industrial work experience from University, now I work part-time as a Receptionist which allows me to continue my studies towards a BA (Hons) in Hospitality Management". Her advice to anyone considering a career in hotels, "Don't be put off by the thought of long hours and less pay initially - I followed my heart when I chose this as a career and I don't regret it for a moment". Michelle hopes to go on to become a Conference and Events Manager when she has completed her degree.

But of course it's not just about hotels - the hospitality industry affects us every day - think about it - grabbing a sandwich for lunch, stopping off for a coffee or drinks with friends, staying at a hotel, going to the cinema or theatre, school meals, eating at a canteen in work, catching a train, motorway service stations... the list goes on and on.......

Claire Rankin is Executive Chef at Fish plc. After studying general catering for 2 years in college her first job was as a chef in a small hotel, before joining Centre Parcs as Commis Chef where she was quickly promoted to Chef de Partie. Moving to London she took a job specialising in fish and within two years became Executive Chef of a new restaurant group - Fish! She says, "My career is very satisfying and I was delighted to be given an industry 'Acorn' award in 2001. My advice to young chefs wanting to progress in their career would be to focus on what they want to achieve - put your head down and keep working. That's what I did - believe me, you will get noticed!"

What about travel and tourism! Sounds great, travel around, see the world, meet people - but is that really all it's about! Well no, of course not, just like any job or career it's what you make it and of course the variety of this sector is enormous. It's a huge growth sector, valued at a massive £270 billion worldwide. In the last 10 years, international tourism has accounted for 1 in 6 of all jobs, 125,000 tourism businesses exist in the UK and 1.75 million people are employed in these businesses.

Travel and Tourism is closely linked with Hospitality and Leisure, all sectors are providing services for their customers. It's a very inter-dependent industry ....it's constantly expanding... which means more jobs and careers!

What's the best way in to this industry then and what qualifications do you need? Hospitality and Catering, like many other sectors, suffer from skills shortages in certain areas. Undoubtedly there are a wide range of jobs on offer-

Receptionists, Bar, Conference and Banqueting, Event Management, Chefs, Waiters, Sales and Marketing, Housekeeping, Food and Beverage Managers ... these are just a few! The three main entry routes are:

By getting a job and benefiting from company training and development-maybe alongside a part-time college course. Whitbread Restaurants offer a fantastic Chef apprentice scheme, which combines training in the work-place with a day-release to College.

By becoming a trainee and securing a Modern Apprenticeship or National Traineeship which will offer full time training for young people up to the age of 25 to NVQ/SVQ level 3.

By enrolling on a full-time college or university course. There are courses to suit all abilities, whatever your academic achievements.

If it's a career in Travel and Tourism that interests you, again there are too many jobs to mention here, Travel Agents, Overseas Reps, Cabin Crew, Marketing for a Tour Operator, Customer Relations, Operations Roles, Cruise Ships, Tourist Information Centres, just a few to consider. This sector is attractive to new recruits and competition can be tough, some of the qualifications that could help you on your way include:

GNVQs unit-based qualifications designed to develop knowledge, skills and understanding in broad vocational areas. These can lead to further/higher education or employment and are available at levels 1 to 3.

NVQs and SVQs. These provide a flexible approach allowing you to progress at your own pace. They have been devleoped to meet real needs of people at work and employers' requirements.

Modern Apprenticeships - an opportunity to develop skills, expertise and gain NVQs whilst at work.

Further and Higher Education - Many universities and some colleges offer HND or degree courses in Travel and Tourism and related subject areas. Often these courses include business studies, field trips, foreign languages and marketing elements.

Qualifications alone are no guarantee of a job in either the hospitality, leisure, travel or tourism industry a lot depends on your personality, attitude, communication skills and - common sense approach to work and life in general.

To find out more contact Springboard UK, who offer career advice on all aspects of the Hospitality, Leisure, Travel and Tourism industry. Their website has loads of information on working in these sectors, with web-links, cv advice, career profiles and a college finder along with information on many of the leading employers so you can find out what is on offer in the way of job prospects, training and career progression.

Hospitality, Leisure and Tourism might not be everyone's choice-but if you are enthusiastic, like people and want a career that's exciting, challenging and constantly developing- contact Springboard UK to check it out - you might just be surprised!

Looking out for a career where every other day is not the same? The hospitality industry is full of excitement and challenges and may be able to offer many a career opportunity. The hospitality industry is one of the fastest growing industries, with a growing number of hotels, B and B, game lodges, clubs, pubs, restaurants, cafeterias and fast food outlets. Careers in the hospitality sector encompass catering services at conferences and meetings, hospitals, prisons, mines, school and university hostels and company canteens.

Hospitality industry offers excellent opportunities for ambitious graduates in functional areas such as operational management, personnel, marketing, sales, finance, training, facilities management, conference management and purchasing. *Hospitality Career* progression is often rapid with companies offering very attractive financial and development recognition for qualified persons.

But aspiring incumbents must bear in mind that the work is physically demanding, especially when you have to be on your feet, serving people who can be hard to please. Still the payoff is worthwhile and you can climb up the career ladder with the right combination of drive and motivation.

Hospitality Career Opportunities: The scope and gamut of the hospitality industry is wide. A major chunk of occupations in the hospitality industry involve service jobs such as housekeeping, maids, linen-room attendants and laundry workers. Others are chefs and cooks, waiters and waitresses, bartenders, food counter workers and various kitchen workers. Some of the career opportunities available in the hospitality sector are listed below:

- Hotel Manager
- Banqueting Manager
- Food and Beverage Manager
- Rooms Division Manager
- Food Services Manager
- Restaurant Manager
- Bartender or Wine Steward
- Executive Housekeeper
- Room Attendant
- Receptionist
- Waiter
- Concierge, porters, bellboys, doorman and valet

Nature of Work: As a manager in restaurant, you will be responsible for extending an enjoyable experience for both vacationing families as well as business travellers. Hotel managers help their guests enjoy a pleasant stay by providing many of the comforts of home, including cable television, fitness equipment and voice mail. In general hotel managers are responsible for ensuring that the operation of their establishments is efficient and profitable.

The managerial duties vary with the size of the hotel. Large hotels will have managers assigned to various departments of the operation, all of whom generally report to the general manger. However, in small hotels, motel or inn with a limited staff, one hotel manager may oversee all aspects of operations.

Resident managers live in the hotels and are on call 24 hours a day to resolve problems or emergencies. In some hotels, the general manager itself acts as a resident manager. The general manager takes care of the overall hotel operations.

Executive house keepers ensure that guest rooms, meeting halls, banquet rooms and public areas are clean, orderly and well maintained. They also schedule and supervise the work of house keepers, inspect rooms and order cleaning supplies.

Front office managers take care of the front office functions, which includes help desk, attending to customer queries and complaints and requests for special services.

The food service operations are taken care of by food and beverages manager. The F_and B manager oversees the restaurants' cocktail lounges and banquet facilities. Some bigger restaurants have convention managers and assistant managers to take care of the day-to-day activities.

In addition bigger hotels have computer operators who maintain and keep track of the guests' bill, reservations, room assignments, meeting and special events. These operators closely work with hotel managers and assistant managers and keep and assist them in the daily activities.

Cookery: Cookery is another major area of work in the hospitality industry. Listed below are some of the career opportunities in the cookery wing of the hospitality industry:

- Head Chef
- Chef
- Sous Chef
- Chef de Parties
- Commis Chef
- Trainee Chef
- Kitchen Porter
- Kitchen Assistant
- Cook
- Catering Assistant

Hospitality Career Qualifications: A degree in hospitality management or related major could fetch you a career in hospitality industry. Most hotels emphasize on specialized training, post-secondary training in hotel or restaurant management for hotel management positions. Many hotels induct fresh graduates with a flair for the service industry and relevant experience.

Internships or part-time or summer jobs are ideal for young aspirants who want a feel of the hospitality industry. Traits most important for success in the hotel and motel industry are good communication skills; the ability to get along with people in stressful situations; a neat, clean appearance; and a pleasant manner.

Work in hotels and other accommodations can be hectic. Hotel staff is expected to process large number of impatient and irate guests with efficiency and equilibrium. Since many hotels function round the clock, careers in the hospitality industry may involve working in varying shifts. Careers in food preparation and food service necessitate working on your feet for long hours. Kitchen workers may need to lift heavy pots and kettles and work near hot ovens and grills. Food service workers need to carry heavy trays of food, dishes and glassware.

Global Career Opportunities in Hospitality

Today there can be few more exciting, challenging and varied career - offering opportunities for fast promotion - than those offered by the hospitality, tourism and leisure industry. This is the world's fastest-growing, job-creating profession.

The hospitality industry has been experiencing a boom time. A plethora of new hotels have been opened; contract catering is becoming an ever-stronger force to be reckoned with; new concepts are abounding; and there is a constant need for top-level industry consultants to advise on the profession as its trans-global expansion continues apace.

One of the many wonderful aspects of this industry is the flexibility and choice it offers. You can start working in hotels and if that doesn't suit, you can change to contract catering or use your experience to go into consultancy, manage a bar, run a restaurant or fast-food outlet, or even aspire to becoming the new Jamie Oliver! If you love action and adventure, then there is the forces' catering sector. If your talents lie in accountancy, then you could become the financial director of a large hotel or catering company. If you are an Information Technology (IT) geek, the profession is in constant need of IT specialists. In short, there is a job to suit just about everyone!

The enormous scope for movement between the industry's many and varied sectors is a vital consideration in view of the uncertainty of today's job market, where the idea of a 'job for life' is rapidly disappearing.

The media has been filled in recent times with stories about more and more people looking for vocational courses, offering better long-term job prospects - a need made even more acute by the fact that the majority of students today have to contribute financially to their tutorial fees. The hospitality and leisure industry undoubtedly provides a very attractive option in this respect.

The profession currently employs one-in-ten people worldwide. A total of 30-35,000 trained people are required at management and supervisory level every year in the UK alone until 2010 to fulfil this potential. The good news for job seekers is that our best estimations currently show that too few students per annum are embarking upon college and university courses. There is therefore an enormous opportunity for thousands of job seekers to pursue rewarding careers in this exciting growth industry.

What is more, the industry is taking itself seriously and planning for the future, with the HCIMA's assistance. This organisation is the London-based worldwide professional body for managers and aspiring managers in the hospitality industry- with a global membership of 23,000. One of our priority objectives is the setting and maintaining of management standards worldwide; and we are constantly seeking to help the hospitality profession maximise its potential through valuing its greatest asset: its management and staff.

Toward this end, the HCIMA introduced in 1998 'Hospitality Assured', the definitive industry standard for delivering customer service excellence. Concerns about low performance of some hotel and catering operators had led the industry to give the HCIMA a mandate to develop 'Hospitality Assured'. To date, over fifty national and international operations have been accredited with the standard. They range from hotel companies - such as Radisson SAS in Malta and de Veer - and food organisations, like Sodexho at British American Tobacco, to famous names in the leisure industry such as Centre Parcs and Warner Holidays.

This scheme-together with the increasing number of hospitality industry businesses seeking 'Investors in People' recognition and other industry-related standards - illustrates the tremendous strides that the profession has taken in becoming an industry of first choice' for potential employees.

However, a criticism often levelled at the hospitality profession is that it involves working long, often unsocial hours. Certainly, a rewarding career in the hotel industry does require a strong personal commitment for those very reasons. But if a person wants to work normal daytime working hours, then the food-service sector provides an ideal option offering tremendous job satisfaction, fast promotion and good financial remuneration. Basically, the industry is whatever you make of its unrivalled career opportunities.

When looking for a college or university that offers the hospitality industry programme most suited to your needs and qualifications, it is vitally important to select an officially accredited course, since there are many of differing quality and industry credibility. At the HCIMA, we have our own accredited courses all over the world. A key past of our work is our word wide benchmarking - the development of a lifetime learning culture for individual managers and potential managers.

In an economic climate where ' adaptability' and 'flexibility' are now key considerations when following a career path, today's managers and aspiring managers are increasingly responsible for their own career development through updating their skills and knowledge. Recognising this fact, we are more conscious than ever of the need to provide support for members - from the time they are students; to the moment they retire from the profession.

For those embarking on a career in the industry, the HCIMA offers a student membership grade for those following accredited programmes of study. For a subsidised subscription, HCIMA

Student Members enjoy services and benefits that will help them complete their programmes of study and find a job upon its completion.

HCMA students Membership includes:

Professional Status: Information - unlimited access to the association's information centre. When faced with an assignment or project, students can get listings and copies of publications press cuttings and journal articles that will help with their projects

Publications - free subscriptions to our management magazine 'hospitality', as well as other HCIMA publications including technical briefing documents and briefing sheets, providing concise information on a whole range of industry topics. Student Members also receive a free welcome pack on joining, full of special offers and useful information.

24-hour access to information via the HCIMA's comprehensive website. There is an exclusive student members help-line;

Unrivalled opportunities to network and make contact with other industry professional, both nationally and internationally, through the association are many events. There is also an opportunity to get more involved by becoming an HCIMA student representative within your college or on your local HCIMA international group committee;

Lifelong career support - HCIMA is on hand to support its members throughout their careers. Upon successful completion of their programmes of study, Student Members can then be upgraded. HCIMA provides a range of job-seeking and support services.

The importance of HCIMA membership cannot be over-emphasised. As more and more university/college graduated flood the job market, the competition has become ever fiercer. Being a member of the HCIMA provides a 'differential' for graduates, since the Hospitality profession perceives Association membership as a benchmark of quality.

We look forward to welcoming international students to the most rewarding career in this exciting, growing profession-offering unsurpassed opportunities to follow a career that suits individual talents and interests.

Hospitality—Apprenticeship

Do you want a rewarding career in a growing industry? Do you want higher pay and benefits and opportunities for advanced education and training?

Skilled people are needed in the Hospitality industry in areas such as culinary/restaurant, catering and hotel operations and supervision. Effective customer service skills are especially important.

Registered Apprentices: The Registered Apprenticeship model is well known and has served the training needs of a variety of businesses and industries over time. The basic components of the model are especially suited to the hospitality industry.

The apprenticeship model helps participants attain high performance through a cohesive process which links formal instruction in the form of a degree or certification with a standardized process of delivering and measuring hands-on/ on-the-job learning (OJL).

For decades, registered apprenticeship programmes have been successful by combining on-the-job learning with classroom theory supported by a strong monitoring component. The apprentice goes through a structured programme established by the employer that includes incremental wage increases until he or she completes the course of training.

How it Works in Hospitality: Training opportunities are provided through vocational courses, community colleges and apprenticeship programmes in food preparation, catering and hotel and restaurant management, offered through restaurant associations and trade unions.

2

Career in Aviation

Overview of the Airline Industry

Significant Points: Although flight crews-pilots and flight attendants-are the most visible occupations, the vast majority of the industry's employees work in ground occupations.

Senior pilots for major airlines are among the highest paid workers in the nation.

A bachelor's degree is increasingly required or preferred for most pilot and flight attendant jobs.

More than 45 percent of workers are members of unions or covered by a union contract.

Nature of the Industry: Air travel in the US grew at a rapid pace until 2001, expanding from 172 million passenger enplanements in 1970 to nearly 615 million in 2000.

However, over the next 3 years, a combination of factors-the events of September 11th, 2001, an economic recession and other factors-combined to reduce traffic back to 1995 levels. Nevertheless, air travel remains one of the most popular modes of transportation.

Airlines in this industry transport passengers and freight over regularly scheduled routes or on routes, called "charters," specifically designed for a group of travellers or a particular cargo. Several classes of airlines function in the United States.

There are 14 major passenger airlines- 11 passenger and 3 all cargo, which the US Department of Transportation defines as having operating revenues of more than $1 billion. The largest of these, often called the "Big Six," generally operate hub-and-spoke systems and also fly internationally.

A hub is a centrally-located airport designated by an airline to receive a large number of its flights from many locations and at which passengers can transfer to flights to any of the locations served by the airline's system. In this way, the greatest number of passengers, from as many locations as possible, can be served in the most efficient way.

In competition with the Big Six are 6 to 10 low-cost low-fare carriers. These carriers have traditionally not used hub and spoke systems and offered flights between limited numbers of cities. They have primarily focused on flying shorter routes (400 miles or less) and on serving leisure travellers. But some low-fare carriers are expanding their routes to include longer transcontinental and nonstop flights. These moves have helped low-fare carriers expand their customer base to include more business travellers.

Another type of passenger airline carrier is the commuter or regional carrier. There are approximately 25 to 30 of these carriers. Regional airlines operate short- and medium-haul scheduled airline service connecting smaller communities with larger cities and with hubs.

Some of the largest regional carriers are subsidiaries of the major airlines, but most are independently owned, often contracting their services to the majors. The regional airlines' fleet consists primarily of smaller 19- to 68-seat turboprop and 30- to 100-seat jet aircraft. The regional airlines are the fastest growing segment of commercial aviation with 1 out of every 8 domestic airline passengers flying on a regional airline during at least part of his or her trip.

Air cargo is another sector of the airline industry. Cargo can be carried in cargo holds of passenger airlines or on aircraft designed exclusively to carry freight. Cargo carriers in this industry do not provide door-to-door service. Instead, they provide only air transport from an airport near the cargo's origin to an airport near the cargo's destination. Companies in the couriers and messengers industry provide door-to-door delivery of parcels either across town or across the continent.

Most sectors of the airline industry were in a downturn in 2002, with several passenger airlines having declared bankruptcy and others on the verge of doing so. After 6 relatively successful years in the late 1990's, fuelled by an increase in passenger volume and a booming economy, the growth in airline passenger traffic began to slow in 2001, coinciding with the economic recession. After the tragic events of September 11, 2001, passenger traffic dropped steeply, causing airlines to cut flights, lay off workers and park surplus aircraft. Although passenger volume has since recovered somewhat, the growth rate in the industry will likely continue to be depressed for several years.

As the low-fare airlines continue to take market share away from the higher cost major airlines and as passenger traffic remains lower, managing costs has become more critical to the survival of some airlines. Labour costs are the airlines' largest cost component-amounting to 38 percent of some airlines' operating costs-and reducing these costs is a key part of the recovery plans of several major airlines.

Because the number of aircraft flight personnel often is fixed by passenger safety regulations, reducing costs usually involves getting the unions representing workers in the air transportation industry to renegotiate their contracts and agree to reduce wages.

The airline industry faces many challenges in the future. Airlines must focus on cost control, cash preservation and cautious growth. The goal of the industry is to be prepared to respond quickly to economic recovery. Passenger volume should slowly improve, but it will take longer for rapid employment growth to return to the air transportation industry.

Working Conditions: Working conditions in air transportation vary widely, depending on the occupation. Although most employees work in fairly comfortable surroundings, such as offices, terminals, or airplanes, mechanics and others who service aircraft are subject to noise, dirt and grease and sometimes work outside in bad weather.

In 2002, the air transportation industry had 11.8 injuries and illnesses per 100 full-time workers, compared with 5.3

throughout private industry. Virtually all work-related fatalities resulted from transportation accidents.

Because airlines operate flights at all hours of the day and night, many workers have irregular hours or variable work schedules. Flight and ground personnel, including mechanics and reservation and transportation ticket agents, may have to work at night or on weekends or holidays.

Flight personnel may be away from their home bases frequently. When they are away from home, the airlines provide them with hotel accommodations, transportation between the hotel and airport and an allowance for meals and expenses. Flight attendants typically fly from 75 to 85 hours a month. In addition to flight time, they have about 50 hours a month duty time between flights.

Flight crews, especially those on international routes, often suffer jet lag-disorientation and fatigue caused by flying into different time zones. Because employees must report for duty well-rested, they must allow ample time to rest during their layovers.

Employment: The air transportation industry provided 559,000 wage and salary jobs in 2002. Most employment is found in larger establishments-nearly 2 out of 3 jobs are in establishments with 1,000 or more workers. However, nearly three-fourths of all establishments employ fewer than 20 workers.

Most air transportation jobs are at major airports located close to cities. A substantial proportion are at airports that serve as central hubs for major airlines.

Occupations in the Industry: Although pilots and flight attendants are the most visible occupations in this industry, almost 70 percent of all employees in air transportation work on the ground in what are called ground occupations.

Two of the largest ground occupations are aircraft and avionics equipment mechanics and service technicians and reservation and transportation ticket agents and travel clerks.

Aircraft and avionics equipment mechanics and service technicians service, inspect and repair planes. They may work on several different types of aircraft, such as jet transports, small propeller-driven airplanes, or helicopters.

Many specialize working on either the airframe (the body of the aircraft), the power-plant (the engines), or avionics (the parts of an aircraft that depend on electronics, such as navigation and communication equipment). In small, independent repair shops, mechanics and technicians usually inspect and repair many different types of aircraft.

Some mechanics and technicians specialize in scheduled maintenance required by the Federal Aviation Administration (FAA). Following a schedule based on the number of hours flown, calendar days, cycles of operation, or a combination of these factors, mechanics inspect the engines, landing gear, instruments and other parts of aircraft and perform necessary maintenance and repairs.

A reservation and transportation ticket agent is most often the first employee passengers meet after entering the airport. Ticket agents work at airport ticket counters and boarding gates and use computers to provide customer service to incoming passengers.

They can make and confirm reservations, sell tickets and issue boarding passes. They also may work in call centres, answering phone inquiries about flight schedules and fares, verifying reservations, issuing tickets and handling payments.

Customer service representatives assist passengers, check tickets when passengers board or disembark from an airplane and check luggage at the reception area and ensure that it is placed on the proper carrier.

They assist elderly or handicapped persons and unaccompanied children in claiming personal belongings and baggage and in getting on and off the plane. They also may provide assistance to passengers who become ill or injured.

Other ground occupations include airplane cargo and freight agents, who take orders from shippers and arrange for transportation of their goods. Baggage handlers, classified under labourers and freight, stock and material movers, hand are responsible for loading and unloading passengers' baggage.

They stack baggage on specified carts or conveyors to see that it gets to the proper destination and also return baggage to passengers at airline terminals. Aircraft cleaners clean aircraft interiors after each flight.

Flight crewmembers make up 31 percent of air transportation employment and include pilots and flight attendants.

Aircraft pilots, co-pilots and flight engineers are highly trained professionals who fly and navigate jet and turboprop airplanes. Generally, the most experienced pilot, or captain, is in command and supervises all other crewmembers.

The pilot and copilot split flying and other duties such as communicating with air traffic controllers and monitoring the instruments. Some aircraft have a third pilot in the cockpit-the flight engineer or second officer-who assists the other pilots by monitoring and operating many of the instruments and systems and watching for other aircraft. Most newer aircraft are designed to be flown without a flight engineer.

Small aircraft and helicopters that transport passengers and cargo and perform activities such as crop dusting, monitoring traffic, fire-fighting and rescue missions are flown and navigated by commercial pilots.

Airline flights must have one or more flight attendants on board, depending on the number of passengers. Their most important function is assisting passengers in the event of an emergency. This may range from reassuring passengers during occasional encounters with strong turbulence to opening emergency exits and inflating escape chutes.

More routinely, flight attendants instruct passengers in the use of safety and emergency equipment. Once in the air, they serve meals and snacks, answer questions about the flight, distribute magazines and pillows and help to care for small children and elderly and disabled persons. They also may administer first aid to passengers who become ill.

The airline industry also relies on many management, professional and administrative support workers to keep operations running smoothly.

Training and Advancement: The skills and experience needed by workers in the air transportation industry differ by occupation. Some jobs may be entered directly from high school, while others require extensive specialized training. Most positions in the airline industry involve extensive customer service contact requiring strong interpersonal and communication skills. Mechanics and pilots require extensive specialized formal training and must be certified by the FAA; skills for many other air transportation occupations can be learned on the job or through company-sponsored training.

Pilots must have a commercial pilot's license with an instrument rating and must be certified to fly the types of aircraft that their employer operates. For example, helicopter pilots must hold a commercial pilot's certificate with a helicopter rating. Pilots receive their flight training from the military or from civilian flying schools. Physical requirements are strict. With or without glasses, pilots must have 20/20 vision and good hearing and be in excellent health. In addition, airlines generally require 2 years of college and increasingly prefer or require a 4-year college degree. Pilots who work for smaller airlines may advance to flying for larger companies. They also can advance from flight engineer to copilot to captain and, by becoming certified, to fly larger planes.

Applicants for flight attendant jobs must be in excellent health. Employers prefer those who have completed some college and have experience in dealing with the public. Speaking a foreign language also is an asset. Airlines operate flight attendant training programmes on a continuing basis.

Training usually lasts from 4 to 8 weeks, depending on the size and the type of carrier. Training may include crew resource management, which emphasizes teamwork and safety. Courses also are provided in personal grooming and weight control. After completing initial training, flight attendants must go through additional training and pass an FAA safety exam each year in order to continue flying.

Advancement opportunities are limited, although some attendants become customer service directors, instructors, or recruiting representatives.

When hiring aircraft mechanics, employers prefer graduates of aircraft mechanic trade schools who are in good physical condition. After being hired, aircraft mechanics must keep up to date on the latest technical changes and improvements in aircraft and associated systems. Most mechanics remain in the maintenance field, but they may advance to head mechanic and, sometimes, to supervisor.

A good speaking voice and a pleasant personality are essential for reservation and transportation ticket agents and customer service representatives. Airlines prefer applicants with experience in sales or in dealing with the public and most require a high school education, but some college is preferred.

Formal company training is required to learn how to operate airline computer systems, issue tickets and plan trips. Some agents and service representatives advance to supervisor or other administrative positions.

Some entry-level jobs in this industry, such as baggage handler and aircraft cleaner, require little or no previous training. The basic tasks associated with many of these jobs are learned in less than a week and most newly hired workers are trained on the job under the guidance of an experienced employee or a manager.

However, promotional opportunities for many ground occupations are limited due to the narrow scope of the duties and the specialized skills of some occupations. Some may advance to supervisor or another administrative position.

Industry Outlook: Wage and salary jobs in the air transportation industry are projected to increase by 12 percent over the 2002-12 period, compared with 16 percent for all industries combined. However, job opportunities may vary from year to year, because the demand for air travel-particularly pleasure travel, a discretionary expense-fluctuates with ups and downs in the economy. In the long run, passenger and cargo traffic is expected to continue expanding in response to increases in population, income and business activity.

Despite a recent slowdown in passenger air travel, demographic and income trends indicate favourable conditions for leisure travel in the United States and abroad over the next decade. The aging of the population, in combination with growth of disposable income among the elderly, should increase the demand for air transportation services.

Also, business travel should improve with the economy and as world trade expands, companies continue to go global and the economies in many foreign countries become more robust. However, as businesses also try to reduce costs, they are resorting to cheaper alternatives to flying and finding new ways to communicate. Many business travellers are using other means of transportation, such as driving or using the railway system, or are conducting more business by phone, e-mail, or better quality and lower cost video-conferencing technologies.

Cargo traffic is expected to increase with the economy and growing world trade. It should also be stimulated by the development of global e-commerce and manufacturing trends such as just-in-time delivery, which requires more materials to be shipped rapidly.

Job opportunities in the air transportation industry are expected to vary depending on the occupation. Pilots and flight attendants are projected to experience average growth through 2012 as the economy and passenger traffic rebound from the severe downturn in the industry.

In the near term, the best opportunities will be with the faster growing regional and low-fare carriers. Persons with a college degree, or former military pilots, can expect to have the best job prospects. Turnover of flight attendants will also produce job openings for this occupation as many leave for more stable work schedules or better salary.

The number of reservation and transportation ticket agents will grow more slowly than the average as airlines phase out paper tickets and move to electronic "ticketless" travel and as more passengers purchase electronic tickets over the Internet. However, the safety and security responsibilities of these jobs will continue, preventing a decline in these jobs. Competition for ticket agent and customer service representative jobs will continue to be keen as many more people are likely to apply for these jobs than there are openings.

Opportunities should be excellent for aircraft and avionics equipment mechanics and service technicians. The likelihood of fewer entrants from the military and a larger number of retirements indicates excellent opportunities for students just beginning technician training.

Opportunities also are expected to be good among unskilled entry-level positions, such as baggage handler and aircraft cleaner, because many workers leave these jobs and need to be replaced.

Airline Careers

When we talk of airline careers, what comes to mind are the glamorous jobs of pilots and flight attendants. But the airline industry functions as a large conglomerate and there are specialized and non-specialized employees that offer their services in various areas. Jobs with airlines could range from security staff, reservations agents and clerical support to marketing personnel and maintenance and cargo handling staff. In the United States, the airline industry is seen as one of the nation's leading growth industries.

It is an industry of big numbers and huge services. We take a look at various careers within the airline industry, in particular the jobs of pilots and flight attendants. Take a peek into what kind of training and schedules these jobs entail. Find out the remuneration and perks that you might enjoy should you take up an airline career.

Airline Industry Career: The airline industry employs men and women with highly diversified skills. The meshing of these varied skills is essential to the operation of every single flight. The mechanics, inspectors and ground service people must make certain aircrafts are completely airworthy and fully prepared for passengers and cargo. Airline pilots need to comply with the strictest employment requirements. This career involves continuous retraining and testing. The flight attendant category represents the largest job sector in the airline industry. Airlines in the US alone employ nearly 80,000 flight attendants. Compensation for desk and runway jobs with an airline would start around $1200 per month. Salaries for airport managers' average around $30,0000 a year. In-flight crew gets better wages and perks that increase with seniority.

A brief of some of the airline jobs:

- Captain-commands the aircraft and is responsible for the safety of its passengers and cargo.
- Copilot-Assists or relieves the captain in the operation of the aircraft.
- Second Officer/Flight Engineer-Assists in flight operations and checks that the mechanical and electronic devices of an aircraft are in perfect working order.
- Flight Attendant (referred to as stewardess or steward) Assures the safety and comfort of passengers during a flight.
- Flight Dispatcher - Authorizes all takeoffs of aircraft and monitors the flight's progress to destination by radio.
- Meteorologist - Prepares reports on weather for flight personnel and for airline operations and traffic departments

Airline support jobs can range from baggage agents to crew schedulers to food service and gate agents and cargo handlers, fuel handlers and maintenance crew.

Pilots: A college degree with major in Aeronautical Science is required of most pilots. A number of colleges and universities offer flight training with credit towards a degree. The graduate may leave school with a Private or Commercial License and/or Flight Instructor's Rating, in addition to a degree. Intensive training is critical to the development of a professional pilot. It is vital to keep abreast of developing trends and newer aircraft models so as to maintain the competitive edge.

- Professional pilots must have extraordinary physical coordination to manoeuvre the aircraft from takeoff to landing, sometimes under confusing and difficult conditions.
- Pilots must be conversant in translating and executing instructions from the ground, which may mean giving further orders to crewmembers.

- Pilots must develop retentive memory to assimilate radio procedures at locations hundreds of miles ahead and be able to apply them to conditions that arise in flight.
- Flight training includes theory and practice. The theoretical phase involves studying the manuals supplied by the flying school. Knowledge of the manuals is tested by written examinations. This testing is required before the FAA issues a pilot's license after certification by the school.

A new pilot may start with a remuneration of around $25,000 a year and will increase with seniority and experience. A captain is given a remuneration of around $130,000 a year. Pilots flying more sophisticated aircrafts are paid more.

Flight Attendant: Typically airlines select flight attendants who are poised and calm, even under duress. Flight attendant candidates are usually around 18 - 25 years of age. Good health, ability to communicate clearly and experience in dealing with people are added skills. Ability to speak a foreign language is an added qualification, especially for international flights. The duties of flight attendants:

- Greeting passengers and helping them to their seats
- Serving beverages and refreshments to the passengers
- Helping the aged or small children who need assistance
- Instructing passengers on use of safety and emergency equipment
- Reporting condition of cabin equipment and any medical problems of any passengers
- Ensuring that first aid kits and emergency equipment is aboard

Flight attendants have to undergo rigorous training ranging from a month to seven weeks. Flight attendants are trained for all emergencies such as CPR, first aid and hijacking. This could also include evacuating an airline, operating emergency systems and equipment and water survival tactics. Flight attendants are trained to understand passenger psychology so as to be better equipped to deal with all types of passengers, including handicapped passengers, unaccompanied minors and unpleasant ones too!

Initially, flight attendants are placed on 'reserve' - they are called to fill in for crewmembers that are sick or on holiday. They are required to report for flights on short notice. The reserve period is usually for a year though it can vary. The work involves working the year round. The monthly working hours are determined by the employees' unions. This airline job involves standing for long hours and working in a pressurized environment, breathing recycled air. This coupled with irregular sleeping and eating patterns leads to medical problems sometimes.

Flight Attendants

Significant Points: Job duties are learned through formal on-the-job training.

Competition for positions will remain strong because the opportunity for travel attracts more applicants than there are jobs, with only the most qualified being hired.

A high school diploma is the minimum educational requirement; however, applicants with a college degree and with experience in dealing with the public are likely to have the best employment opportunities.

Nature of the Work: Major airlines are required by law to provide flight attendants for the safety of the travelling public. Although the primary job of the flight attendants is to ensure that safety regulations are followed, attendants also try to make flights comfortable and enjoyable for passengers.

At least 1 hour before each flight, attendants are briefed by the captain—the pilot in command—on such things as emergency evacuation procedures, coordination of the crew, the length of the flight, expected weather conditions and special issues having to do with passengers. Flight attendants make sure that first-aid kits and other emergency equipment are aboard and in working order and that the passenger cabin is in order, with adequate supplies of food, beverages and any other provided amenities. As passengers board the plane, flight attendants greet them, check their tickets and tell them where to store carry-on items.

Before the plane takes off, flight attendants instruct all passengers in the use of emergency equipment and check to see that seatbelts are fastened, seat backs are in upright positions and all carry-on items are properly stowed. In the air, helping passengers in the event of an emergency is the most important responsibility of a flight attendant. Safety-related actions may range from reassuring passengers during rough weather to directing passengers who must evacuate a plane following an emergency landing.

Flight attendants also answer questions about the flight; distribute reading material, pillows and blankets; and help small children, elderly or disabled persons and any others needing assistance. They may administer first aid to passengers who become ill. Flight attendants generally serve beverages and other refreshments and, on many flights, heat and distribute precooked meals or snacks. Prior to landing, flight attendants take inventory of headsets, alcoholic beverages and moneys collected. They also report any medical problems passengers may have had, the condition of cabin equipment and lost and found articles.

Lead, or first, flight attendants, sometimes known as pursers, oversee the work of the other attendants aboard the aircraft, while performing most of the same duties.

Working Conditions: Because airlines operate around the clock and year round, flight attendants may work nights, holidays and weekends. In most cases, agreements between the airline and the employees' union determine the total daily and monthly working time.

Scheduled on-duty time usually is limited to 12 hours per day although some contracts provide daily actual maximums of 14 hours, with somewhat greater maximums for international flying. Attendants usually fly 65 to 90 hours a month and, in addition, generally spend about 50 hours a month on the ground preparing planes for flights, writing reports following completed flights and waiting for planes to arrive. They may be away from their home base at least one-third of the time. During this period, the airlines provide hotel accommodations and an allowance for meal expenses.

Flight attendants must be flexible, reliable and willing to relocate. However, many flight attendants elect to live in one place and commute to their assigned home base. Home bases and routes worked are bid for on a seniority basis. The longer the flight attendant has been employed, the more likely he or she is to work on chosen flights. Almost all flight attendants start out working on reserve status or on call. On small corporate airlines, flight attendants often work on an as-needed basis and must adapt to varying environments and passengers.

The combination of free time and discount airfares provides flight attendants the opportunity to travel and see new places. However, the work can be strenuous and trying. Flight attendants stand during much of the flight and must remain pleasant and efficient, regardless of how tired they are or how demanding passengers may be. Occasionally, flight attendants must deal with disruptive passengers. Also, turbulent flights can add to possible difficulties regarding service, including potential injuries to passengers.

Working in a moving aircraft leaves flight attendants susceptible to injuries. For example, back injuries and mishaps can occur when opening overhead compartments or while pushing heavy service carts. In addition, medical problems can arise from irregular sleeping and eating patterns, dealing with stressful passengers, working in a pressurized environment and breathing recycled air.

Training, Other Qualifications and Advancement: Airlines prefer to hire poised, tactful and resourceful people who can interact comfortably with strangers and remain calm under duress. Applicants usually must be at least 18 to 21 years old, although some carriers may have higher minimum-age requirements. Flight attendants must have excellent health and the ability to speak clearly. All US airlines require that applicants be citizens of the United States or registered aliens with legal rights to obtain employment in the United States.

Airlines usually have physical and appearance requirements. There are height requirements for reaching overhead bins, which often contain emergency equipment and most airlines want candidates with weight proportionate to height. Vision is required to be correctable to 20/30 or better with glasses or contact lenses (uncorrected no worse than 20/200). Men must have their hair cut above the collar and be clean shaven. Airlines prefer applicants with no visible tattoos, body piercing, or unusual hairstyles or makeup.

A high school diploma is the minimum educational requirement. However, airlines increasingly prefer applicants with a college degree and with experience in dealing with the public. Applicants who attend schools and colleges that offer flight attendant training may have an advantage over other applicants. Highly desirable areas of concentration include people-oriented disciplines such as psychology and education. Flight attendants for international airlines generally must speak a foreign language fluently. For their international flights, some of the major airlines prefer candidates who can speak two major foreign languages.

In addition to education and training, airlines conduct a thorough background check as required by the FAA, which goes back as many as 10 years. Everything about an applicant is investigated, including date of birth, employment history, criminal record, school records and gaps in employment. Employment is contingent on a successful background check. An applicant will not be offered a job or will be immediately dismissed if his or her background check shows any discrepancies.

Once hired, all candidates must undergo a period of formal training. The length of training, ranging from 3 to 8 weeks, depends on the size and type of carrier and takes place at the airline's flight training centre. Airlines that do not operate training centres generally send new employees to the centre of another airline. Some airlines may provide transportation to the training centres and an allowance for room, board and school supplies, while other airlines charge individuals for training. New trainees are not considered employees of the airline until they successfully complete the training programme. Trainees learn emergency procedures such as evacuating an airplane, operating emergency systems and equipment, administering first aid and surviving in the water. In addition, trainees are taught how to deal with disruptive passengers and with hijacking and terrorist situations. New hires learn flight regulations and duties, gain knowledge of company operations and policies and receive instruction on personal grooming and weight control. Trainees for the international routes get additional instruction in passport and customs regulations. Trainees must perform many drills and duties unaided, in front of the training staff. Throughout training, they also take tests designed to eliminate unsuccessful trainees. Toward the end of their training, students go on practice flights. Upon successful completion of training, flight attendants receive the FAA's Certificate of Demonstrated Proficiency. Flight attendants also are required to go through periodic retraining and pass an FAA safety examination to continue flying.

After completing initial training, flight attendants are assigned to one of their airline's bases. New flight attendants are placed on reserve status and are called either to staff extra flights or to fill in for crewmembers who are sick, on vacation, or rerouted. When they are not on duty, reserve flight attendants must be available to report for flights on short notice. They usually remain on reserve for at least 1 year, but, in some cities, it may take 5 to 10 years or longer to advance from reserve status. Flight attendants who no longer are on reserve bid monthly for regular assignments. Because assignments are based on seniority, usually only the most experienced attendants get their choice of assignments. Advancement takes longer today than in the past because experienced flight attendants are remaining in this career longer than they used to.

Some flight attendants become supervisors or take on additional duties such as recruiting and instructing. Their experience also may qualify them for numerous airline-related jobs involving contact with the public, such as reservation ticket agent or public-relations specialist.

Employment: Flight attendants held about 102,000 jobs in 2004. Commercial airlines employed the vast majority of flight attendants, most of whom lived in their employer's home-base city. A small number of flight attendants worked for large companies that operated aircraft for business purposes.

Job Outlook: In the long run, opportunities for persons seeking flight attendant jobs should improve as the airline industry continues to recover from the effects of September 11, 2001 and the downturn in the economy. Employment of flight attendants is expected to grow about as fast as average for all occupations through the year 2014. Population growth and an improving economy are expected to boost the number of airline passengers. As airlines expand their capacity to meet rising demand by increasing the number and size of planes in operation, more flight attendants will be needed. Over the next decade, however, demand for flight attendants will fluctuate with the demand for air travel, which is highly sensitive to swings in the economy. During downturns, as air traffic declines, the hiring of flight attendants declines and some experienced attendants may be laid off until traffic recovers.

Despite the improving outlook, competition is expected to be keen because this job usually attracts more applicants than there are jobs, with only the most qualified eventually being hired. College graduates who have experience dealing with the public should have the best chance of being hired. Job opportunities may be better with the faster growing regional and commuter, low-fare and charter airlines. There also are job opportunities for professionally trained flight attendants to work for companies operating private aircraft for their executives.

The majority of job openings through the year 2014 will arise from the need to replace flight attendants who leave the labour force or transfer to other occupations, often for higher earnings or a more stable lifestyle. With the job now viewed increasingly as a profession, however, fewer flight attendants leave their jobs and job turnover is not as high as in the past. The average job tenure of attendants is currently more than 7 years and is increasing.

Earnings: Median annual earnings of flight attendants were $43,440 in May 2004. The middle 50 percent earned between $31,310 and $67,590. The lowest 10 percent earned less than $23,450 and the highest 10 percent earned more than $95,850.

According to data from the Association of Flight Attendants, beginning attendants had median earnings of about $15,552 a year in 2004. Beginning pay scales for flight attendants vary by carrier, however. New hires usually begin at the same pay scale regardless of experience and all flight attendants receive the same future pay increases based on an established pay scale. Flight attendants receive extra compensation for increased hours. Further, some airlines offer incentive pay for working holidays, night and international flights, or taking positions that require additional responsibility or paperwork. Most airlines guarantee a minimum of 65 to 85 flight hours per month, with the option to work additional hours. Flight attendants also receive a "per diem" allowance for meal expenses while on duty away from home. In addition, flight attendants and their immediate families are entitled to free or discounted fares on their own airline and reduced fares on most other airlines. Some airlines require that the flight attendant be with an airline for 3 to 6 months before taking advantage of this benefit. Other benefits may include medical, dental and life insurance; 401K or other retirement plan; sick leave; paid holidays; stock options; paid vacations; and tuition reimbursement.

Flight attendants are required to purchase uniforms and wear them while on duty. The airlines usually pay for uniform replacement items and may provide a small allowance to cover cleaning and upkeep of the uniforms. The majority of flight attendants hold union membership, primarily with the Association of Flight Attendants. Other unions that represent flight attendants include the Transport Workers Union of America and the International Brotherhood of Teamsters.

Minimum Qualifications to Become a Flight Attendant

Am I Qualified?

One of the first steps in evaluating a flight attendant career is determining whether you qualify for the position. Every airline has a set of minimum hiring requirements.

Education: Virtually every airline requires that you have a high school degree or Government Equivalency Degree (GED) If you did not finish high school or have not passed the GED, do not bother to apply for a job as a flight attendant. You absolutely won't get hired without a high school degree (or equivalent).

When you review each airline's minimum hiring qualifications, you should realize that these are merely minimums. More is always better, especially when it comes to education. Just because you have a high school degree, do not expect to walk into an airline employment office, show your diploma and get hired.

Many airlines look favorably upon applicants who have tried to better themselves by pursuing higher education. A recent study shows that over one-half of all flight attendants hired have at least one year of college under their belt and over one-third have an Associate's or Bachelor's degree. A few even have Master's degrees or Doctorate's; these types of advanced degrees are certainly not required for the job, but will be helpful if you plan on pursuing a management or supervisory position someday.

Additionally, if you are lacking customer service experience, many airlines will overlook this "weakness" if you have a college education behind you. Hiring departments believe that college experience makes applicants more mature and better able to handle the many challenges and responsibilities that come with being a flight attendant.

Customer Service Experience: Customer service experience is typically not a firm requirement; meaning, you can usually apply without it. However, a lack of customer service experience makes getting hired that much more difficult. Customer service experience will give you a clear competitive advantage in your quest to become a flight attendant.

Remember that you will be working in front of the public on a regular basis. From greeting, serving and assisting passengers to making announcements, you will always be representing the company in a customer service role. Because it is very important to project a positive image, airlines are very careful about selecting candidates who have experience working with the public.

Most people do not even realize that they have a customer service background. If you have ever worked in an environment in which you had to deal with the public on a regular basis, you have customer service experience. This can include working in a retail clothing store, waiting tables in a restaurant, answering telephones in a corporate environment, etc.

However, if you do not have any customer service experience, you should not despair. You may have a more difficult time than others who do, but it won't preclude you from landing the job, especially if you excel in other qualification areas. For example, the airlines will usually substitute a college education (even without a degree) for a lack of customer service experience.

Language Skills: Fluency in a second language, such as French, Spanish, German, Japanese, or Chinese is a major plus in the eyes of flight attendant hiring departments; however, most airlines are only concerned with your ability to speak English. Fluency in English is a must. If you cannot speak English effectively, you won't get hired by a US airline.

Very few airlines require you to be able to speak a second language. Airlines that have a second language preference do so because of certain international destinations. On these routes, a designated Language of Destination/Origin (also called LOD/O - pronounced "low-doe") flight attendant is assigned to the flight. Such positions are usually awarded to senior flight attendants, making these jobs difficult to obtain even for qualified applicants. Pay is also higher for LOD/O qualified flight attendants - approximately $1.50 to $2.00 higher per hour.

Citizenship: Every major US airline requires you to be a US Citizen or registered alien with legal right to accept employment in the US, plus the right to travel to and from the countries the airline serves.

You are also required to have a social security card and, in many instances, a passport. If you do not have a passport, it might be a good idea to get one now. They take just a few weeks to obtain.

Relocation: Every major airline requires that you be willing to relocate to any of the listed flight attendant domiciles.

Appearance: The airlines are very particular about hiring individuals who have a neat and attractive appearance. After all, flight attendants are the only employees to have direct, continuous contact with the travelling public. No matter what the marketing department propagates over the airwaves or in print, flight attendants must look neat and professional in order for the airline to develop an appealing brand identity.

Typically, airlines do not permit visible tattoos, body piercings (save for your ears), long hair on men, "rebellious" hairstyles, bizarre or offensive-looking makeup or jewellery, poorly manicured hands, etc. All airlines are different. For example, some do not even permit facial hair on men! During training, you will be given specific grooming regulations which must be strictly adhered to.

Company Physical and Background Check: If you have thoroughly read through the minimum hiring requirements (above), you may be thinking it would be easy enough to "cheat" a little bit during the application process - maybe say you are a year older or an inch taller than you actually are, or fail to mention that DWI conviction you had three years ago. You do not want to do this, trust us! Airlines have a couple of ways to determine whether applicant have lied on their application about their age, height, past use of drugs, work history, or any other area that would preclude them from landing the job.

Every airline administers a company physical examination to every new-hire. During this exam, an airline is able to detect whether you lied on your application about your height, whether you have a drug or alcohol problem, or whether your past medical history shows anything adverse that would disqualify you from getting the job. Since you are given a urinalysis during this physical, it is very important that you inform the examiners of any medications you might be taking.

In addition to the medical exam, there is also a thorough background check. During the background check, which can go back as many as 10 years, virtually everything about you is investigated - your age, place of birth, school records, criminal records (if any), etc. If an airline finds that you lied on your application or you have any sort of criminal record, you will be immediately dismissed

What to expect from Flight Attendant Training?: Anxiety about new-hire flight attendant training is common once the euphoria of getting hired wears off. Don't worry! You will be trained by professionals on everything you need to know.

Once hired, candidates must undergo a period of formal training. The length of training, ranging from 4 to 7 weeks, depends on the size and type of carrier and takes place in the airline's flight training centre.

Flight attendant training usually takes place at the airline's training centre and typically lasts from three to six weeks. Classes are usually made up of between 30 and 100 trainees and run from approximately 8:00AM to 4:30PM.

Airlines that do not operate flight attendant training centres generally send new employees to the centre of another airline. Airlines may provide transportation to the training centres and an allowance for board, room and school supplies. However, new trainees are not considered employees of the airline until they successfully complete the training programme.

Trainees learn emergency procedures such as evacuating an airplane, operating emergency systems and equipment, administering first aid and water survival tactics. In addition, trainees are taught how to deal with disruptive passengers and hijacking and terrorist situations. New hires learn flight regulations and duties, company operations and policies and receive instruction on personal grooming and weight control. Trainees for the international routes get additional instruction in passport and customs regulations.

Other subjects covered during flight attendant training typically include: City Codes, 24-hour clock, Time computations adding/subtracting hours and minutes), Airline terminology, Cabin service, Company policy and procedures, Aircraft

Familiarization, First Aid/CPR, Ditching, Evacuation drills/ commands, Security/Bomb threats, Uniform regulations, FARs, Bidding/Reserve, Specific aircraft training, non-specific aircraft training and much more.

Towards the end of their training, students go on practice flights. You can also expect about 4 training flights with real passengers where you will perform your duties under the supervision of working flight attendants.

Generally you will be given tests after each segment of flight attendant training. Passing grades are typically 90%. Some airlines allow retakes. Some do not. It might also be helpful to practice airport codes (pick up a schedule) and practice adding time. You can check your answers by using the hours and minutes calculator that we have added to the site.

During the second or third week, you will be asked to fill out your "dream sheet" for base assignments which will be awarded later in the programme, depending upon the needs of the airline. After completing initial training, flight attendants are assigned to one of their airline's bases.

Additionally, flight attendants must receive 12 to 14 hours of annual training in emergency procedures and passenger relations.

What about Flight Attendant Training Academies?: We receive quite a number of e-mails asking whether it is beneficial to attend a flight attendant training academy.

We do not recommend attending any of these schools and we have no significant proof that it helps in the application and hiring process. These schools can cost as much as $3,000 for several weeks of intense training, but much of the training is not airline specific, so procedures you might be learning will not be the same as you will learn in your airline's new-hire training programme.

We also have questions about what type of college one should attend to be better prepared for the flight attendant profession. Our answer here is that although a college degree is not required by most airlines, the years you spend there could work in your favour (even if you don't graduate). That is because some airlines will substitute up to two years of college for one's lack of customer service experience. If you were to pick a major or course of study, we would recommend becoming fluent in a second language. That is the number one attribute that will put you head and shoulders above the competition at many airlines.

The bottom line here is that airlines will train you in everything you need to know, so there is no need to try to do it on your own. The hardest part of the job is getting hired and anything you can do to tilt the odds in your favour will help. A second language, customer service experience, or prior flight attendant employment are all positive attributes.

Flight Attendant Salaries: Median annual flight attendant salaries were $38,820 in 2000. The middle 50 percent earned between $28,200 and $56,610. The lowest 10 percent earned salaries of less than $18,090 and the highest 10 percent earned more than $83,630. According to data from the Association of Flight Attendants, beginning median flight attendant salaries were about $14,847 a year in 2000.

Unlike most 9 to 5 office workers who earn salaries that are privately negotiated and performance-based, flight attendant salaries are paid an hourly union rate that is based almost entirely on seniority.

For example, all first year flight attendant salaries at a particular airline might be $19 per hour; all sixth year flight attendants, $32 per hour; and all fourteenth year flight attendants, $41 per hour.

Each airline's hourly base rate is unique. Some airlines pay higher hourly rates than others. It all depends on the labour contract. Every 3 to 5 years, each airline negotiates a new labour contract with its flight attendant union. Once compensation is agreed upon, it is fixed for the duration of the contract.

Calculating Flight Attendant Salaries: As a flight attendant, you won't be paid this hourly rate for every hour that you work. The time you spend commuting to the airport, sleeping in hotel rooms, standing around the airport between flights and assisting passengers during boarding and deplaning is essentially unpaid labour.

Most airlines only pay you from the time an aircraft pushes back from the gate to the time it arrives at the gate of its destination. This is commonly referred to as flight time, block time, or hard time. The major exception to this is meal expenses. Most airlines pay a nominal hourly rate to cover meal expenses. Hotel lodging is paid for by the airline.

Technically, flight attendants are paid based on accrued pay time, which includes block time plus any excess claim time. Claim time is time paid in excess of block time. For example, if you were required to deadhead to another city during a trip, you would not work the flight (and would not earn block time), but would be entitled to additional deadhead time. This additional time would be reflected in your pay time.

Instead of flight time-based pay, certain airlines compensate flight attendants based on the number of accrued monthly flight miles. Others pay flat salaries regardless of the hours (or miles) flown. These compensation methods are unique, but you should nevertheless be aware of them.

Flight Attendant Salaries Vary for Other Reasons: Job performance has virtually no impact on your pay. You are expected to work at a high level and will never receive a bonus or promotion of any kind, even for exemplary service. This may seem a little strange to you, especially if you have spent a portion of your life in an office building trying to climb the corporate ladder.

On the positive side, since pay is tied directly to seniority, you will receive guaranteed annual pay raises; they are built right into the contract. As a new-hire, you might even receive a mandatory pay raise after only 6 months of employment, immediately following the probationary period. Another positive aspect of unionized labour is that it eliminates much of the jealousy and biases that surround compensation in corporate America.

For example, you will never hear someone say, "I wonder what they are paying him?, or "I know they are not paying me what I'm worth because I'm a minority." After all, seniority determines pay, which cannot be influenced by human prejudices. On the negative side, however, you are essentially at the mercy of the labour contract and have no negotiating power as an individual when it comes to compensation. If you believe you are underpaid, you cannot exactly walk into your supervisor's office and ask for more money. Instead, you must rely on your union representatives to stand up for you - and every other flight attendant who works for the airline - during contract negotiations.

Since you cannot negotiate pay as a flight attendant, be sure to choose an airline that makes the most financial sense before accepting employment. You will want to choose an airline that is in an active hiring mode. This will help you gain seniority more quickly, resulting in better pay. You should also choose an airline with competitive flight attendant salaries. Granted contracts change every 3 to 5 years, but typically frugal airlines stay frugal and more generous ones stay generous. If you want to make the most amount of money, stick to the major airlines.

To a certain extent, any flight attendant can simply peruse the labour contract to determine what a fellow employee is earning. After all, if you know someone's date of hire, you can easily determine their hourly rate; it is in the contract! You must realize, however, that although flight hour base rates are fixed, actual monthly income can vary even between flight attendants with comparable seniority.

For example, some airlines offer premium flight attendant salaries for those who work the lead or "A" flight attendant position, work at night or on certain weekends and holidays, or fly international flights. Additionally, the number of flight hours a flight attendant chooses to fly in a given month has a dramatic affect on income. Certain airlines have a two-tiered wage system which also affects how much you can earn as a flight attendant.

Air Hostess

Be an Air Hostess 2pm Delhi, 6pm Mumbai, 10pm Calcutta... If this is what you'd fancy your jet-setting travel schedule to be, plus you'd like to get paid for it, then the airlines may be just the kind of job that you are looking for.

You must be A 12th standard pass, but a Bachelors degree is preferable, between 19-27 years with a minimum height of 5'3 for girls and 5'7 for boys and not more than 6'0. While it is a popular career choice for girls, boys can also work as pursers which requirers which requiruage to know). If selected you will be on training for 2 months in which time you learn about service, grooming, safety and first aid, after which you are initially put on 10 trainee flights.

The working hours depend on the sector you are allotted, which means that you may have to work night shifts at times. The max number of work hours per week generally does not extend to more than 30hrs. The entry level salary in domestic airlines is in the range of Rs 12,000 and can go to a max of Rs 20,000. International airlines pay packet may be anywhere between Rs 20,000 to Rs 40,000. That's not too bad whether you're fresher or someone with work experience. Airlines usually require that air-hostesses sign a bond of 3-5 yrs.

Career Prospects: One can move into other areas such as Ground hostess, Catering and Quality Control. One could also move up the ladder in 2 years and get into management as well as training of airhostesses. Airlines looking for you Jet Airways is known to recruit frequently and most freshers have landed a job with them and then moved on to other domestic or International airlines, like Singapore Airlines.

International airlines which have regular flights from India recruit Indian hostesses & stewards, though they often prefer to take those with experience on the domestic sector.

Middle East, Gulf Air, Emirates etc. take many Indian girls but it is said that passengers, many of whom are not very well educated, can be difficult to handle. Cathay Pacific was a major recruiter before the Asian financial crisis forced the company to downsize its operations.

Air India/ Indian Airlines being a government organisation has permanent employees on the roster who never seem to retire (air hostesses fly till they're 55!) and sizeable SC/ST reservation. So chances of joining are right now somewhat dim. Ads for recruitment normally appear in all major publications, so keep a lookout!

The Down Side: While most girls are lured by the glamour factor, remember the job demands a lot of hard work and odd working hours which may affect your social/ family life. Frequent travelling and jet lag sometimes take their toll on health. However most airlines shift you to a ground job by the time you're 35. Even tho statistics say a person is more likely to die in a car accident than in an air crash, the element of risk is always there.

You could be faced with an emergency situation like a hijack. Neerja Bhanot, an air hostess on board the ill fated Panam flight hijacked at Karachi airport in 1986 lost her life, even as she saved countless passengers on board with her extraordinary courage and presence of mind. She was posthumously awarded the Ashok Chakra, India's highest civilian award for bravery. Experienced air-hostesses complain of getting bored doing the same job day after day and say that you must have high levels of energy. If you feel that you can handle the stress, possess a lot of patience to deal with annoying passengers (at times) and love meeting people then happy flying.

It's the age of the jumbo and the jet-set. Everybody wants to be in the sky these days; from a statesman, to the family next door taking for their annual holiday.

They fly in aircraft in which a high standard of safety and service are first priorities. Among those helping to provide service are the stewardesses, girls who combine the efficiency of a first-class secretary with the charm of a diplomat. Their job demands many qualities, including a capacity for hard work and an ability to keep calm in an emergency.

An Air Hostess is indeed the mistress of all she surveys inside an aircraft during flights. Inside the aircraft, she is the one who seems to be here, there and everywhere, greeting every passenger with a smile, elegantly guiding each to his or her seat, generously helping a passenger get settled, coordinating security personnel, giving directions to the caterers and doing a myriad things. In most cases it is the girls who prefer this career although boys can do the same job as stewards.

Eligibility: More or less all airlines have a set standard of selection criteria for Air Hostess. An Air Hostess aspirant is expected to be proficient in the required languages (usually English, Hindi and one foreign language) and a graduate in any subject or diploma holder in hotel management from a recognized university / institute.

You should be between 19 and 26 years of age, with a height of at least 157.5 centimeters, with your weight proportionate to your height as per the standards set. Eligibility for an Indian Passport, unmarried status and perfect eyesight and health are other important factors considered as well as a clear complexion and a pleasing personality.

After initial screening, the candidate will have to qualify written test and subsequent group discussions and interviews. During training you will be taught the guidelines and necessary procedures and for safety and services, etc. Apart from the physical and other attributes mentioned above, you should also have a lot of stamina, patience, common sense, presence of mind and the strength to keep yourself poised in the face of a crisis. An outgoing personality and a bit of luck always help.

Age: 18 - 25

Qualification: Minimum +2 or a hotel management degree or a graduate degree

Height: 157.5 cms (without slippers or shoes)

Weight: in proportion with height

Marital Status: Unmarried

Complexion: Fair to clear

Normal Eyesight: No specs (6/24 - uncorrected normal vision (distant) in each eye)

Job Prospects: Starting off as an Air Hostess, you have to take progressive examinations for promotions and attend the refresher courses to keep abreast of the latest technology. There is every chance that you can then be promoted to the post of Senior Flight Attendant and then Head Attendant.

Your career as an Air Hostess would last for about eight to ten years, after which you could move on to the ground duties including the job of a Ground Hostess, Check Hostess, etc. or diversify into any one of the other departments in the airline industry.

With privatisation and foreign collaboration increasing every day, the future is bright for an Air Hostess. Most airline offices are looking to increasing their fleet and there is a demand for Air Hostesses. While it is a fact that most airline offices prefer to advertise when they plan to recruit, candidates may send their resume, along with a photograph, to airline offices on their own initiative.

Flight Steward

Looking for a Career Option as a member of Cabin Crew (Air Hostess/Flight Steward)? This section features Air Hostess/ Flight Steward as a career option, elaborated with reference to the job profile, personality traits required, the courses and training involved, premier institutions and future prospects.

The air hostess and/or flight steward (also referred to as cabin crew), are the first people to welcome passengers aboard an aircraft. They welcome and greet every passenger. They help them to supervise their seating arrangements and help them in arranging their hand baggage in the proper manner. Once all the passengers have come in they set about ensuring the safety-belt arrangements and demonstrate the use of emergency equipment. They make the necessary announcements over the public address system. Their duties and responsibilities start much before the arrival of the passengers by checking that blankets, pillows, magazines, newspapers, etc. are in good order in their proper places.

Air hostesses and flight stewards have to be on duty throughout the duration of the flight looking after passengers in general and taking special care of air-sick travellers, sick children and babies; and also the elderly people or very young who are travelling alone. They provide first aid should the situation arise. They serve meals to passengers and crew and after the meal clear the dishes and check again that all passengers have been served all the items. They work continuously and efficiently during the flight in the confined space of the cabin with a good humour.

Depending on the routes they fly, cabin crew may get to do a lot of sightseeing; the longer the route the higher are the chances of sightseeing as crews often change planes at 'slip points' or step overs. At these times they stay at luxury hotels at the airlines' expense.

Personality Traits: Common sense a sense of responsibility, ability to handle crisis, initiative, helpful, friendly nature, physical stamina and the capacity to work with speed and efficiency, systematic approach, attractive appearance, a well modulated pleasant voice and a proportionate figure with good posture and bearing are important traits for cabin crew.

Eligibility: Airlines recruit cabin crew (air hostess/ flight stewards) on the basis of certain eligibility criteria:

1. Age: Below 25 years
2. Height: Minimum height should be 154.5-157.5 cm (barefeet) for air hostess and 170-180 cms for flight steward
3. Weight: Proportionate to height as per the company's standards
4. Status (marital): Unmarried
5. Vision: Preferably normal eyesight without glasses; or minimum uncorrected vision (distant) should be 6/24 in each eye.
6. Educational: Graduate degree from a recognised university, or Plus Two/Equivalent with 3 year diploma in Hotel Management and Catering from a recognised institute.
7. Knowledge of the national language and at least one international language (English) is essential.
8. The applicant should be physically fit with a pleasing personality and clear complexion.

Courses/Training: After completing the initial screening of applicants private airlines company may invite them for a written examination, usually of the objective type (multiple choice). Those who qualify in the written test have to appear for a group discussion followed by a personal interview of successful candidates.

Trainee cabin crew undergo training in catering, first aid, general airborne procedures, documentation (dealing with the flight documents they have to complete after each flight), use of the public address system and technical details of aircraft pressurization and ventilation. They are given lessons in the use of safety equipment and the emergency drill. At first the practical work is taught on firm ground; later on they have to gain flight practice flying as an extra or supernumerary.

Institutions:

- Air Hostess Flight Steward Colleges in Kerala (1)
- Air Hostess Flight Steward Colleges in New Delhi (5)

Placements and Prospects: With privatisation and many international airlines flying to Indian destinations, cabin crew are being recruited not just by the domestic airlines, but also by foreign airlines. The different airlines advertise their openings. The different airlines include private owned domestic and international airlines namely Sahara, Singapore airlines, Jet Airways etc. and government air services like Air India and Indian Airlines. Interested candidates must keep a lookout for the advertisements and apply as per the specifications. A resume accompanied by a photograph in a walk-in interview to the recruiting airline.

An Air Hostess has every chance to be promoted to the post of Senior Flight Attendant and then Head Attendant. Career as an Air Hostess would last for about eight to ten years, after that she could move on to the ground duties including the job of a Ground Hostess, Check Hostess, training of airhostess or work in the management level. One can also diversify into any one of the other departments in the airline industry.

The span of their flying career as symbols of hospitality may tend to be contractual, but experienced cabin crew are successfully absorbed in alternative careers in travel and tourism, hotels and in mass media, to name a few prominent options.

Job Description: The Air Hostess's work begins from the moment the plane taxic down the tarmac and pulls up in front of the aerobridge. She's at the aircraft door, warm smile on her face, welcoming passengers on board. She guide them to their seats and helps them with their luggage.

Once the plane is in full flight, she rolls out the cart-load of goodies, food and drinks, chocolates and coffee, snacks and tea.

Often passengers have qyeries, some of which can be quite trivial. Its for three Air Hostess to field these. She ensures that the flight commander's instructions are carried out, doors are barred and seat belts fastened. She also instructs them about the different safety and emergency rules, as well as the medical help is looked after by herself only.

There have been instances of Air Hostesses displaying valour and even laying down their lives for the safty of passengers. The Air Hostess knows the aircraft layout like the back of her hands and can evacuate passengers real fast from plane in the time of crisis.

Eligibility: To become an Air Hostess you don't need any special academic qualification. A graduation in any subject will do. There are, however, some carriers which insist on a diploma in either hotel or tourism management. But what you really need to make a mark in this field is a mix of right personality, aptitudes, skills and attitudes. One other thing that the most airlines insist on is that the candidate must not be married at the time of appointment.

You definitely get an adge if you are fluent in a foreign language other than English. An Air Hostess needn't to be beautiful, but glamorous and charming she must be, a height of 160 cm and well groomed look are important.

Prospects: Depending on which airline you join, your starting pay could range between Rs 16,000 and 35,000 a month. Senior Air Hostess, both in Indian Airline and Air-India, draw as much as Rs.75,000 per month. Domestic private airlines pay even better and a senior Air Hostess with a foreign carrier draws up to an equivalent of Rs. three lakhs a month.

The airlines usually advertise in the appointments columns of the leading English language dailies. In the year, there can be two or three such advertisements, if not more. You may also try your luck, sending in forced applications to the airlines. The Air Hostess work on flights till she is around 38, after which she is transferred to other department, such as ticketing.

Corporate giants such as the Tatas, Relience and the Mahindras have their own jets. They too recruit Air Hostesses. But such appointments are rare.

Where to Apply in India:

- Indian Airlines: Air India Building, 218 Nariman Point, Mumbai- 400 021
- Air India: Air India Building, 218 Nariman Point, Mumbai-400 021
- Jet Airways: 41-42 Maker's Chambers III, Nariman Point, Mumbai-400 021
- Sahara India Airlines: Ambadeep, 14 K.G Marg, New Delhi-110 001
- Jagson Airlines Ltd: Vandana Building, 11, Tolstoy Marg, New Delhi-110 001
- British Airways: D L F Centre, Sansad Marg, New Delhi-100 001
- Cathay Pacific: Tolstoy House, Tolstoy Marg. New Delh-110 001
- Lufthansa Airlines: Express Towers, Nariman Point, Mumbai-400 021
- Emirates Airlines: Mittal Chambers, Nariman Point, Mumbai-400 021
- Delta Airlines: C-37, East Of Kailash, NewDelhi-110065
- You may also go to a grooming school to train as an Air Hostess:
- Birla Institute of Futuristic Studies: M.B Girls High School, 17, Darga Road, Calcutta-700017

How do you start a career as a flight attendant? The airline industry is a highly competitive business and only those well-prepared will make it past the first interview.

A recent report by the Bureau of Labour commented that "in the long run, opportunities for persons seeking flight attendant jobs should improve as the airline industry recovers from the aftereffects of September 11 and the downturn in the economy."

Employment of cabin crew is expected to grow about as fast as the average for all occupations through the year 2012. Population growth and an improving economy are expected to boost the number of airline passengers.

As airlines enlarge their capacity to meet rising demand by increasing the number and size of planes in operation, more flight attendants will be needed. However, over the next decade, one can expect that demand for cabin crew will fluctuate with the demand for air travel, which is highly sensitive to swings in the economy. During downturns, as air traffic declines, the hiring of flight attendants declines and some experienced attendants may be laid off until traffic recovers.

Despite the improving outlook, competition is expected to be keen because this job usually attracts more applicants than there are jobs, with only the most qualified eventually being hired.

The majority of job openings through the year 2012 will arise from the need to replace those who leave the labour force or transfer to other occupations, often for higher earnings or a more stable lifestyle.

However, with the job now viewed increasingly as a profession, fewer are leaving their jobs and job turnover is not as high as in the past. The average job tenure of attendants is currently more than 7 years and is increasing.

Cabin Crew Jobs offers you detailed information about how to successfully launch your career in half the time, with half the hassle.

Equipment Mechanics and Service Technicians

Significant Points: Most workers learn their job in 1 of about 170 schools certified by the Federal Aviation Administration (FAA).

Job opportunities should be excellent for persons who have completed an aircraft mechanic training programme, but keen competition is likely for the best paying airline jobs.

Job opportunities are likely to be the best at small commuter and regional airlines, at FAA repair stations and in general aviation.

Nature of the Work: To keep aircraft in peak operating condition, aircraft and avionics equipment mechanics and service technicians perform scheduled maintenance, make repairs and complete inspections required by the Federal Aviation Administration (FAA).

Many aircraft mechanics, also called airframe mechanics, power plant mechanics and avionics technicians, specialize in preventive maintenance. They inspect aircraft engines, landing gear, instruments, pressurized sections, accessories—brakes, valves, pumps and air-conditioning systems, for example—and other parts of the aircraft and do the necessary maintenance and replacement of parts. They also maintain records related to the maintenance performed on the aircraft. Mechanics and technicians conduct inspections following a schedule based on the number of hours the aircraft has flown, calendar days since the last inspection, cycles of operation, or a combination of these factors.

In large, sophisticated planes equipped with aircraft monitoring systems, mechanics can gather valuable diagnostic information from electronic boxes and consoles that monitor the aircraft's basic operations. In planes of all sorts, aircraft mechanics examine engines by working through specially designed openings while standing on ladders or scaffolds or by using hoists or lifts to remove the entire engine from the craft. After taking an engine apart, mechanics use precision instruments to measure parts for wear and use x-ray and magnetic inspection equipment to check for invisible cracks. They repair or replace worn or defective parts.

Mechanics also may repair sheet metal or composite surfaces; measure the tension of control cables; and check for corrosion, distortion and cracks in the fuselage, wings and tail.

After completing all repairs, they must test the equipment to ensure that it works properly.

Mechanics specializing in repair work rely on the pilot's description of a problem to find and fix faulty equipment. For example, during a preflight check, a pilot may discover that the aircraft's fuel gauge does not work. To solve the problem, mechanics may troubleshoot the electrical system, using electrical test equipment to make sure that no wires are broken or shorted out and replace any defective electrical or electronic components. Mechanics work as fast as safety permits so that the aircraft can be put back into service quickly.

Some mechanics work on one or many different types of aircraft, such as jets, propeller-driven airplanes and helicopters. Others specialize in one section of a particular type of aircraft, such as the engine, hydraulics, or electrical system. *Airframe mechanics* are authorized to work on any part of the aircraft except the instruments, power plants and propellers. *Powerplant mechanics* are authorized to work on engines and do limited work on propellers. *Combination airframe-and-powerplant mechanics*—called A&P mechanics—work on all parts of the plane except the instruments. Most mechanics working on civilian aircraft today are A&P mechanics. In small, independent repair shops, mechanics usually inspect and repair many different types of aircraft.

Avionics systems are now an integral part of aircraft design and have vastly increased aircraft capability. *Avionics technicians* repair and maintain components used for aircraft navigation and radio communications, weather radar systems and other instruments and computers that control flight, engine and other primary functions. These duties may require additional licenses, such as a radiotelephone license issued by the US Federal Communications Commission (FCC). Because of the increasing use of technology, more time is spent repairing electronic systems, such as computerized controls. Technicians also may be required to analyze and develop solutions to complex electronic problems.

Working Conditions: Mechanics usually work in hangars or in other indoor areas. When hangars are full or when repairs must be made quickly, they can work outdoors, sometimes in unpleasant weather. Mechanics often work under time pressure to maintain flight schedules or, in general aviation, to keep from inconveniencing customers. At the same time, mechanics have a tremendous responsibility to maintain safety standards and this can cause the job to be stressful.

Frequently, mechanics must lift or pull objects weighing more than 70 pounds. They often stand, lie, or kneel in awkward positions and occasionally must work in precarious positions, such as on scaffolds or ladders. Noise and vibration are common when engines are being tested, so ear protection is necessary. Aircraft mechanics usually work 40 hours a week on 8-hour shifts around the clock. Overtime work is frequent.

Training, Other Qualifications and Advancement: Most mechanics who work on civilian aircraft are certified by the FAA as an "airframe mechanic" or a "powerplant mechanic." Mechanics who also have an inspector's authorization can certify work completed by other mechanics and perform required inspections. Uncertified mechanics are supervised by those with certificates.

The FAA requires at least 18 months of work experience for an airframe or powerplant certificate. For a combined A&P certificate, at least 30 months of experience working with both engines and airframes is required. Completion of a programme at an FAA-certified mechanic school can substitute for the work experience requirement. Applicants for all certificates also must pass written and oral tests and demonstrate that they can do the work authorized by the certificate. To obtain an inspector's authorization, a mechanic must have held an A&P certificate for at least 3 years, with 24 months of hands on experience. Most airlines require that mechanics have a high school diploma and an A&P certificate.

Although a few people become mechanics through on-the-job training, most learn their job in 1 of about 170 trade schools certified by the FAA. About one-third of these schools award 2-year and 4-year degrees in avionics, aviation technology, or aviation maintenance management.

FAA standards established by law require that certified mechanic schools offer students a minimum of 1,900 actual class hours. Coursework in schools normally lasts from 18 to 24 months and provides training with the tools and equipment used on the job. Aircraft trade schools are placing more emphasis on technologies such as turbine engines, composite materials—including graphite, fiberglass and boron—and aviation electronics, which are increasingly being used in the construction of new aircraft. Additionally, employers prefer mechanics who can perform a variety of tasks.

Some aircraft mechanics in the Armed Forces acquire enough general experience to satisfy the work experience requirements for the FAA certificate. With additional study, they may pass the certifying exam. In general, however, jobs in the military services are too specialized to provide the broad experience required by the FAA. Most Armed Forces mechanics have to complete the entire training programme, although a few receive some credit for the material they learned in the service. In any case, military experience is a great advantage when seeking employment; employers consider applicants with formal training to be the most desirable applicants.

Courses in mathematics, physics, chemistry, electronics, computer science and mechanical drawing are helpful because they demonstrate many of the principles involved in the operation of aircraft and knowledge of these principles is often necessary to make repairs. Courses that develop writing skills also are important because mechanics are often required to submit reports.

FAA regulations require current work experience to keep the A&P certificate valid. Applicants must have at least 1,000 hours of work experience in the previous 24 months or take a refresher course. As new and more complex aircraft are designed, more employers are requiring mechanics to take ongoing training to update their skills. Recent technological advances in aircraft maintenance necessitate a strong background in electronics—both for acquiring and for retaining jobs in this field. FAA certification standards also make ongoing training mandatory. Every 24 months, mechanics are required to take at least 16 hours of training to keep their certificate. Many mechanics take courses offered by manufacturers or employers, usually through outside contractors.

Aircraft mechanics must do careful and thorough work that requires a high degree of mechanical aptitude. Employers seek applicants who are self-motivated, hard working, enthusiastic and able to diagnose and solve complex mechanical problems. Agility is important for the reaching and climbing necessary to do the job. Because they may work on the tops of wings and fuselages on large jet planes, aircraft mechanics must not be afraid of heights.

Advances in computer technology, aircraft systems and the materials used to manufacture airplanes have made mechanics' jobs more highly technical. Aircraft mechanics must possess the skills necessary to troubleshoot and diagnose complex aircraft systems. They also must continually update their skills with and knowledge of new technology and advances in aircraft technology.

As aircraft mechanics gain experience, they may advance to lead mechanic (or crew chief), inspector, lead inspector, or shop supervisor positions. Opportunities are best for those who have an aircraft inspector's authorization. In the airlines, where promotion often is determined by examination, supervisors sometimes advance to executive positions. Those with broad experience in maintenance and overhaul might become inspectors with the FAA. With additional business and management training, some open their own aircraft maintenance facilities. Mechanics learn many different skills in their training that can be applied to other jobs and some transfer to other skilled repairer occupations or electronics technician jobs. Mechanics with the necessary pilot licenses and flying experience may take the FAA examination for the position of flight engineer, with opportunities to become pilots.

Employment: Aircraft and avionics equipment mechanics and service technicians held about 142,000 jobs in 2004; about 5 in 6 of these workers was an aircraft mechanic and service technician. More than half of aircraft and avionics equipment mechanics and service technicians worked for air transportation companies. About 18 percent worked for the Federal Government and about 14 percent worked for aerospace products and parts manufacturing firms. Most of the rest worked for companies that operate their own planes to transport executives and cargo. Few mechanics and technicians were self-employed.

Most airline mechanics and service technicians work at major airports near large cities. Civilian mechanics employed by the US Armed Forces work at military installations. Mechanics who work for aerospace manufacturing firms typically are located in California or in Washington State. Others work for the FAA, many at the facilities in Oklahoma City, Atlantic City, Wichita, or Washington, DC. Mechanics for independent repair shops work at airports in every part of the country.

Job Outlook: Opportunities for aircraft and avionics equipment mechanics and service technicians should be excellent for who have completed aircraft mechanic training programmes. Employment is expected to increase about as fast as average for all occupations through the year 2014 and large numbers of additional job openings should arise from the need to replace experienced mechanics who retire.

Reduced passenger traffic—resulting from a weak economy and the events of September 11, 2001—forced airlines to cut back flights and take aircraft out of service. However, over the next decade passenger traffic is expected to increase as the result of an expanding economy and a growing population and the need for aircraft mechanics and service technicians will grow accordingly. Furthermore, if the number of graduates from aircraft mechanic training programmes continues to fall short of employer needs, opportunities for graduates of mechanic training programmes should be excellent.

Most job openings for aircraft mechanics through the year 2014 will stem from replacement needs. Many mechanics are expected to retire over the next decade and create several thousand job openings per year. In addition, others will leave to work in related fields, such as automobile repair, as their skills are largely transferable to other maintenance and repair occupations. Also contributing to favourable future job opportunities for mechanics is the long-term trend toward fewer students entering technical schools to learn skilled maintenance and repair trades. Many of the students who have the ability and aptitude to work on planes are choosing to go to college, work in computer-related fields, or go into other repair and maintenance occupations with better working conditions. If the trend continues, the supply of trained aviation mechanics will not be able to keep up with the needs of the air transportation industry.

Job opportunities are likely to be the best at small commuter and regional airlines, at FAA repair stations and in general aviation. Commuter and regional airlines are the fastest growing segment of the air transportation industry, but wages in these companies tend to be lower than those in the major airlines, so they attract fewer job applicants. Also, some jobs will become available as experienced mechanics leave for higher paying jobs with the major airlines or transfer to another occupation. At the same time, general aviation aircraft are becoming increasingly sophisticated, boosting the demand for qualified mechanics. Mechanics will face more competition for jobs with large airlines because the high wages and travel benefits that these jobs offer generally attract more qualified applicants than there are openings. Also, there is an increasing trend for large airlines to outsource aircraft and avionics equipment mechanic jobs overseas; however, most airline companies prefer maintenance work done on aircraft be performed in the US because of safety and regulation issues of overseas contractors.

In spite of these factors, job opportunities with the airlines are expected to be better than they have been in the past. But, in general, prospects will be best for applicants with experience. Mechanics who keep abreast of technological advances in electronics, composite materials and other areas will be in greatest demand. Also, mechanics who are mobile and willing to relocate to smaller rural areas will have better job opportunities. The number of job openings for aircraft mechanics in the Federal Government should decline as the government increasingly contracts out service and repair functions to private repair companies.

Job opportunities for avionics technicians who are prepared to master the intricacies of the aircraft and work with A&P mechanics are expected to be good. Technicians who are cross-trained and able to work with complex aircraft systems should have the best job prospects. Additionally, technicians with licensing that enables them to work on the airplane, either removing or reinstalling equipment, are expected to be in especially high demand.

Earnings: Median hourly earnings of aircraft mechanics and service technicians were about $21.77 in May 2004. The middle 50 percent earned between $17.82 and $27.18. The lowest 10 percent earned less than $13.99 and the highest 10 percent earned more than $33.84. Median hourly earnings in the industries employing the largest numbers of aircraft mechanics and service technicians in May 2004 were:

Scheduled air transportation	$27.37
Federal Government	21.67
Nonscheduled air transportation	20.88
Aerospace product and parts manufacturing	20.60
Support activities for air transportation	18.70

Median hourly earnings of avionics technicians were about $21.30 in May 2004. The middle 50 percent earned between $18.12 and $25.12. The lowest 10 percent earned less than $14.63 and the highest 10 percent earned more than $27.85.

Mechanics who work on jets for the major airlines generally earn more than those working on other aircraft. Airline mechanics and their immediate families receive reduced-fare transportation on their own and most other airlines.

About 4 in 10 aircraft and avionics equipment mechanics and service technicians are members of unions or covered by union agreements. The principal unions are the International Association of Machinists and Aerospace Workers and the Transport Workers Union of America. Some mechanics are represented by the International Brotherhood of Teamsters.

Aviation Maintenance Technology

Programmes in aviation maintenance technology prepare people to repair and maintain airplanes and helicopters. Students learn to repair and maintain engines. They also learn how to service ignition systems and electronic instruments. They learn to build and repair frames and fittings.

Are you nervous on airplanes? You shouldn't be. The only form of transportation that's safer than an airplane is an elevator. And this is largely because of the careful maintenance that airplanes get. Federal laws mandate regular inspections, tests and service routines. And the people who do the maintenance have to meet strict federal licensing requirements.

If you want to be one of those licensed technicians, you need to complete a training programme approved by the Federal Aviation Administration (FAA). The programme usually takes two to three years of full-time study and training beyond high school. About 150 schools offer this programme. Some of these schools are colleges. And in some you can get the training as part of a two-year programme that awards you an associate degree.

The training programmes are designed to prepare you for the licensing exams. Therefore, the subjects you study in these programmes do not vary much from one school to another. You study the structure of airplanes and the various metallic and nonmetallic parts. You learn how to inspect and repair structural parts. You also study the parts of the engines and how they function. You learn about schedules for inspection and for routine servicing. You practice repairing engines and testing the results. Depending on your career goal, you may want to specialize in the structure or the engines. Most airlines prefer you to be certified in both.

You may also study the electronics of aircraft. If you've ever seen a picture of an airplane cockpit, surely you've noticed the dozens of switches, dials and lights. Aircraft use electronics to control the engines, to steer and to navigate. They also use it to track weather, to communicate and to monitor all onboard systems. When you study avionics you learn how to troubleshoot and repair these systems. You learn the basics of electronic circuits and then study the specialized systems used in aircraft. Fewer than 100 schools offer this programme.

With experience and authorization from the FAA, you can be an inspector. This allows you to perform required inspections and certify the work of other mechanics."

College Preparation: Proprietary schools, colleges and universities all offer this programme. If you want to study at a proprietary school, you can prepare for this programme of study by completing your high school degree or getting a GED. If you want to study at a college or university, you can prepare for this programme by taking the following courses: four years of English, three years of math, three years of social studies and two years of science. Some colleges also require two years of a second language.

Computer Science and Programming

Technical Writing

Principles of Technology

Algebra

Concentrations

You may specialize in maintaining the airframe - that is, the body of the aircraft. You may specialize in maintaining the powerplant - that is, the engines. You may specialize in avionics- that is, the electronics. You may combine airframe and powerplant ("A & P"). Or, you may combine one or even both with avionics.

Typical Course Work

A certificate programme for both airframe and powerplant typically includes courses in the following subjects:

- Aircraft Drawing
- Aircraft Electrical Systems
- Aircraft Materials and Their Inspection
- Aircraft Structures: Nonmetallic
- Aircraft Structures: Sheet Metal
- Basic Electricity

- Engine Cooling, Lubrication and Inspection
- Engine Fuel Metering Systems
- Engine Ignition Systems
- Engine Induction and Exhaust Systems
- Federal Regulations, Records and Publications
- Gas Turbine Engines: Installation, Operation, Overhaul
- Instrument, Control and Warning Systems
- Landing Gear, Hydraulic and Pneumatic Systems
- Propeller Systems
- Reciprocating Engines: Installation, Operation, Overhaul
- Technical Mathematics

A certificate programme in avionics technology typically includes courses in the following subjects:

- AC Circuits
- Airframe and Engine Systems Interfacing
- College Algebra
- Communication and Navigation Basic Circuits
- DC Circuits
- Digital Applications
- Introduction to Avionics
- Navigation Systems
- Operational Testing of Aircraft Electronic Systems

Things to Know

To work in this field as anything other than an assistant, you need FAA certification. This may qualify you as an "airframe mechanic," "powerplant mechanic," or "avionics repair specialist. You need at least 18 months of work experience to sit for the exam for any one of these. If you want the combined "A & P" (airframe and powerplant), you need 30 months of experience. Completing an FAA-approved training programme substitutes for that experience.

If you want to work in avionics, it helps to get a general radiotelephone operator license. The Federal Communications Commission (FCC) issues this license. You need to pass an exam to get it.

Your next career move may be to become an inspector. To be authorized for that, you need to hold the A&P certification for at least three years.

You will need to take classes to keep your skills up-to-date with changing technology. The FAA recognizes this and requires a certain minimum number of hours every two years. Most employers also recognize this and pay for you to take classes.

Aviation Operations and Services

Programmes in aviation operations and services prepare people to manage flight operations. Students learn to manage airports and ground traffic. They also learn flight safety and security. They study air traffic regulations and business practices.

Nearly everyone has been to an airport at least once. Even if there isn't a long line at the ticket counter, there's always lots of activity to watch. Planes land and take off during every hour of the day, especially at America's busiest airports. Besides the pilots and flight attendants attending the planes, it takes many people to keep airports running 24 hours a day, seven days a week.

Aviation operations programmes teach people about the aviation industry. In addition to learning how airplanes work, you learn how airports operate. You also study how companies make different kinds of aircraft. You learn business skills as well as technical information, from FAA (Federal Aviation Administration) regulations to meteorology.

With a degree in aviation operations, you can work for public and private airports and government agencies such as the FAA. You can also work for commercial airline companies, private companies, or airplane manufacturers. You can help direct planes in and out of airports, create plans to market new planes to airline companies, or analyze ways airports can be more efficient.

In aviation operations programmes, you take courses from different areas, including business, aeronautical science and communications. Your business courses are usually about management techniques, accounting, economics and labour relations. You also take courses about flight safety, airport operations and the structure of airline companies. Your courses will teach you basic business skills and how to apply them specifically to the aviation industry.

Many two-year schools offer associate degrees in aviation operations and services. Several four-year schools offer bachelor's degree in the field. Two-year programmes prepare you for base-level positions while a bachelor's degree prepares you for entry-level management positions. In some cases, a two-year degree can be transferred to a four-year school.

Master's degrees in this field are in the broader area of aviation or aviation management. The focus of these programmes is less hands-on. Instead, graduate programmes are geared more towards the theory and oversight of aviation services."

College Preparation: For this programme schools recommend that you know how to use a computer and the Internet. You can prepare for this programme by taking courses in high school that prepare you for college. This typically includes four years of English, three years of math, three years of social studies and two years of science. Some colleges also require two years of a second language.

Business Computer Applications

Advanced English Composition courses

Business and Applied English

Advanced Chemistry courses

Physics

Calculus

Graduate Admissions

Admission to graduate programmes is competitive. You need a bachelor's degree in aviation (or a significant amount of course work in aviation or a similar field), good grades and good test scores

Additional requirements at some schools include:

- Graduate Record Exam (GRE) General

- Letters of recommendation
- Personal statement

Typical Course Work: This undergraduate programme typically includes courses in the following subjects:

- Accounting
- Air Navigation
- Air Traffic Control
- Aircraft Systems
- Airline Administration
- Airport Management and Planning
- Aviation History
- Aviation Labour Relations
- Aviation Law
- Computer Science
- Economics of Air Transportation
- Flight Safety
- Group Communication
- Human Resource Management
- Introduction to Aeronautics
- Marketing
- Meteorology
- Operations Management
- Physics
- Statistics

Graduate study in aviation operations and services typically includes:

- Required courses
- Thesis (master's degree)

Things to Know

Although not required, many programmes encourage you to get your pilot's certificate.

Aviation operations programmes are sometimes called "aviation administration" or "aviation services.

Air Traffic Control

Programmes in air traffic control prepare people to direct air traffic. Students learn to use radar and radio communication to talk to pilots. They learn to read flight plans, instruments and weather conditions. They also get hands-on experience at an FAA (Federal Aviation Administration) flight control center during training.

Have you ever felt that someone was watching you, but couldn't see who it was? You just couldn't shake that feeling. Pilots probably feel that way all the time, but in their case, it's a good thing! Air traffic controllers watch the moves of pilots as they fly planes in and out of airports. They also minimize traffic delays and make sure planes are a safe distance apart in the air and that it is safe to take off or land.

When you think of air traffic controllers, you probably think about the people sitting in the tower at the airport. While many air traffic controllers work in control towers, there are several different types of air traffic controllers. Many work at different stations in airports and in air traffic control centres across the country. Air traffic controllers also perform many different tasks. Depending on your location, you might control takeoff and landing, aircraft maintenance, or the flight time after takeoff. Some controllers watch rather than direct air traffic. They provide information on routes and weather to pilots and controllers. They help other air traffic controllers do their job well by looking at general flight patterns.

About 15 schools offer air traffic control programmes. These range from certificate and two-year associate degree programmes to bachelor's degree programmes. All of these programmes offer background preparation for students who wish to become air traffic controllers. In these programmes, you study the airway system, FAA rules, aircraft performance and related job skills. You learn to use controller equipment, including computers, radar and electronic communication.

Throughout your training, you must pass several exams. You must also show that you can spot and solve problems quickly. In addition, you also must show that you know how to apply FAA procedures and rules to many air traffic situations.

In addition, the FAA provides 15-17 weeks of intense training in air traffic control at its academy in Oklahoma City for people who meet their strict admission requirements. This training is followed by several years of successful on-the-job experience and is required for employment as an air traffic controller."

College Preparation

Courses that emphasize computer skills, spatial relationships and oral communication are essential.

You can prepare for this programme by taking courses in high school that prepare you for college. This typically includes four years of English, three years of math, three years of social studies and two years of science. Some colleges also require two years of a second language.

General Computer Applications

Computer Technology

Aviation

Public Speaking

Undergraduate Special

Before you can go to the FAA training academy, you must first be admitted to an FAA-approved air traffic control programme. Once admitted to a programme, you must pass a pre-employment test given through the FAA. Passing this test means you have the right set of skills to become an air traffic controller.

When you successfully finish the programme, you then attend the FAA training academy in Oklahoma City. However, there are several additional requirements that you must meet:

- You must have three years of general work experience, four years of college, or a combination of the two
- Be 30 years old or younger
- Be a US citizen
- Be able to speak, read and write English well
- Pass several medical and psychological exams and a background check

Typical Course Work

This programme typically includes courses in the following subjects:

- Air Traffic Control
- Basic Air Navigation
- Basic Meteorology
- Business
- Communications Procedures
- Engineering
- Interpretation of Weather Conditions
- Mathematics
- Science

Many of your classes will include simulation time. This means that you use computers and radar equipment to learn concepts. You pretend to monitor air traffic and communicate with pilots. This tests your on-the-job skills.

Things to Know

Nearly all air traffic controllers work for the government. Most work for the Federal Aviation Administration, although some work for the Department of Defense. A few work for private companies.

Controllers must pass a physical exam each year, so they must be in good shape.

Controllers must also pass a job performance exam at least once per year.

College graduates with civilian or military experience as controllers, navigators, or pilots have the best chances of entering the air traffic controller programme.

College Preparation: To qualify for a commercial pilot's license, applicants must:

- Be at least 18 years old
- Be able to speak, read, write and understand English
- Hold a private pilot's certificate
- Have at least 250 hours of flight experience

- Pass a strict physical exam
- Have 20/20 vision with or without glasses
- Have good hearing
- Pass written exams on safe flight and navigation techniques
- Demonstrate their flying abilities to FAA examiners

Typical Course Work

This programme typically includes courses in the following subjects:

- Advanced Aerodynamics
- Advanced Flight Maneuvers
- Advanced Night Flying
- Advanced Weather
- High-Performance Takeoffs and Landings

Many programmes teach students flight maneuvers using a flight simulator. This is in addition to flight time with an instructor.

Things to Know

Being a commercial pilot isn't very different from being a private pilot. The main advantage is that you are allowed fly an airplane and carry passengers and/or cargo for money. However, there are many regulations about doing this, depending on who owns the plane, how large the plane is and other considerations.

You can also study for advanced ratings on your commercial pilot's license. This means that you can become rated to fly using instrument flight rules. You can also learn to fly planes with more than one engine. To achieve an advanced rating, pilots must take additional hours of instruction and pass exams.

All licenses remain valid as long as pilots can pass the periodic physical exams and tests of flying skills.

Many people who want to become a pilot for an airline also become a flight instructor. This is because airlines require that you fly a large number of hours before you can work for them.

Being a flight instructor allows you to log the hours you spend training others while getting paid for your time.

Private Pilot

Private pilot programmes teach people how to fly airplanes and helicopters. Students learn ground rules, radio operation and safety. They prepare to take FAA (Federal Aviation Administration) license exams.

Have you ever dreamt that you were flying? For some, it's scary. For others, it's liberating to zoom through the air and look at the earth below as you speed along. If the thought of flight gives you a thrill, you'll be happy to know that it's surprisingly easy to get your private pilot's license.

Private pilot programmes usually consist of ground courses and in-flight training. The ground course prepares you to take a knowledge test. You learn the basics about flying, including aerodynamics, types of aircraft and flight instruments. You also learn about weather, navigation and how airports work.

Once you have passed the knowledge test, you can begin flight training. This consists of renting a plane and buying flight lessons from an FAA-approved flight instructor. You learn how to determine a plane's proper weight and balance, fuel requirements and altitude. You also learn how to take off and land, decide proper runway lengths and prepare your plane for a flight. In addition, you learn how to make good decisions while flying during difficult weather and situations.

FAA regulations state that you must complete a minimum of 40 hours of flight training. These hours include 20 hours with an instructor and 10 hours of flying solo. Of these hours, you must fly certain distances (cross-country) and at night. You must also complete several successful takeoffs and landings and use your instruments. Your flight instructor will teach you all these things during your lessons.

Once you have completed the ground course and passed the knowledge test and flight training, your instructor then "endorses" your logbook. This means that you have met the requirements and successfully can pilot your plane. Then, as long as you are 17, you can take the practice test. During the test, the examiner asks you questions that you must answer orally. You also demonstrate all aspects of flying an airplane. This includes preparing the plane for flight, taking off, using your instruments correctly and landing.

The practical test must be given by an FAA-designated examiner.

Ground courses are offered by private flight schools, community colleges, high schools, four-year colleges and universities and through ROTC training. You can also self-study for the knowledge test by buying textbooks and materials through the Internet and private companies.

You can take flying lessons from private flight schools, independent flight instructors and some community colleges. Many people learn to fly through military service. The length of flight training varies depending on the type of school, the type of flight training and the student's ability to learn the required knowledge and skills."

College Preparation: To qualify for a private pilot's license, applicants must:

- Be at least 16 years old to fly solo
- Be able to speak, read, write and understand English
- Obtain a basic medical certificate
- Have 20/40 vision, with or without glasses
- Pass written exams on safe flight and navigation techniques
- Demonstrate your flying abilities to FAA examiners

Associate degree programmes usually require at least a high school diploma for admission."

Typical Course Work

This programme typically includes courses in the following subjects:

- Aeronautical Charts
- Aeronautical Information Publications
- Aircraft Operations
- Communications Procedures

- Engine Operation
- Federal Aviation Regulations
- Flight Instruments
- Flight Theory
- Interpretation of Weather Conditions
- Navigation Theory
- Radio Communications

Many programmes teach students flight maneuvers using a flight simulator in addition to flight time with an instructor. Once you show sufficient skill and confidence, you can fly the aircraft by yourself.

Things to Know

You can be any age to begin flight instruction. However, you must be at least 17 to get your private pilot's license.

The private pilot's license must be earned before a student may begin training for a commercial pilot's license.

Requirements and health restrictions become stricter if you decide you want to be a commercial pilot.

Your pilot's license never expires. However, you must complete a flight review every two years.

3

Career in Hotel Industry

Hotel Management

What is Hotel Management?: It is exactly what it suggest– the bringing of professional management techniques to that specialist sector of the services industry – the hospitality sector.

Demand: The hospitality industry has grown by leaps and bounds in the past decade and its still growing. Demand for manpower in this industry therefore is immense. Star hotels require trained staff for all these departments:

- Food and beverage (F&B)
- Housekeeping
- Accounting
- Marketing
- Recreation
- Computer Applications
- Financial management
- Engineering
- Maintenance
- Security
- Fire fighting
- Public relations.

Hotel Manager

Hotel managers keep everything in a hotel running smoothly, from ensuring that staff are working well to keeping control of supplies and budgets, looking after the accommodation, food and drink and perhaps the entertainment and conference facilities. Managers have to ensure that guests are comfortable and enjoy their stay. In a large hotel, the hotel manager may lead a team of managers, each responsible for a section such as housekeeping, maintenance, or food and beverages. In a small hotel, the manager is more involved in the day-to-day running of the business, coping with whatever arises, from carrying guests' luggage to pouring drinks or dealing with minor repairs.

Entry Level: To join a management trainee scheme with a large hotel or hotel group, you would normally need at least an HNC/HND in a relevant subject or even a degree or postgraduate qualification. Relevant degrees include hospitality management and international hospitality management, hotel and catering management and hotel, tourism and licensed retail management. Business degrees - perhaps including hospitality, tourism or marketing - are another option.

The minimum qualifications for a degree are usually two A levels/Advanced Highers/three H grades and five GCSEs/S grades (A-C/1-3), or equivalent. For BTEC/SQA HNCs/HNDs, one A level/Advanced Higher/two H grades and four GCSEs/S grades (A-C/1-3) or equivalent qualifications would normally get you in.

If you already have a degree in another subject, you can take a one-year conversion course in hotel and catering management or a graduate apprenticeship.

Some people start work lower down the career ladder, working towards NVQs/SVQs or studying part time for a Hotel and Catering International Management Association (HCIMA) Advanced Certificate in Hospitality Studies. For this, you would need at least two years' relevant experience and should already be working at supervisory level in the industry.

Making the Grade: Much of the training is on the job and involves gaining experience in different areas of the business. You may be encouraged to take specialised courses in areas such as finance, marketing, human resources, food safety and training.

Some hotel managers take postgraduate courses, which can help with career progress. If you want to develop your business skills to a very high level, the Master of Business Administration (MBA) is a popular option in the hospitality industry.

Personal Qualities: As a hotel manager, you would need a good head for business, the ability to motivate and lead staff, an aptitude for figures and excellent organisational skills. You must be able to work well in a team, to think on your feet and to be friendly, helpful and tactful with guests.

A smart appearance and an outgoing personality would be essential and some foreign language skills would certainly be an asset.

Looking Ahead: Although there is fierce competition for the best posts, there are usually lots of opportunities for hotel managers in what is still a growing industry. Your promotion prospects would depend on the size of the hotel and your skills and experience: it could take several years to work through posts such as assistant front-of-house manager to deputy manager and then manager.

With suitable experience, there is always the prospect that you could eventually open your own hotel.

Alternative Suggestions: You might also consider catering manager, chef, human resources officer/manager, leisure services manager, marketing executive or public relations officer. The Hospitality and Catering or Leisure and Tourism industries present Global Opportunities.

Take-home Pay: There is a wide range of salaries, according to the size and type of hotel and your level of responsibility. You might start as a trainee hotel managers on around £12,000 to £14,000, rising to £16,000 to £25,000 as a deputy manager and £40,000 or more for an experienced general manager.

Other benefits might include profit-sharing, performance bonuses and live-in accommodation.

Effects: Hotel managers tend to work long hours, including evenings, nights, weekends and public holidays. They may work in shifts.

The advantages of living in the hotel itself can be outweighed by the inconvenience of being called on to help with problems or make decisions even when you are not on duty.

Hotel, Motel and Resort Desk Clerks

Significant Points: Job opportunities should be plentiful, because of substantial replacement needs.

Evening, weekend and part-time work hours create potential for flexible schedules.

Professional appearance and personality are more important than formal academic training in landing a job.

Nature of the Work: Hotel, motel and resort desk clerks perform a variety of services for guests of hotels, motels and other lodging establishments. Regardless of the type of accommodation, most desk clerks have similar responsibilities. They register arriving guests, assign rooms and check out guests at the end of their stay. They also keep records of room assignments and other registration-related information on computers. When guests check out, desk clerks prepare and explain the charges, as well as process payments.

Front-desk clerks always are in the public eye and typically are the first line of customer service for a lodging property. Their attitude and behaviour greatly influence the public's impressions of the establishment. And as such, they always must be courteous and helpful. Desk clerks answer questions about services, checkout times, the local community, or other matters of public interest. Clerks also report problems with guest rooms or public facilities to members of the housekeeping or maintenance staff for them to correct the problems. In larger hotels or in larger cities, desk clerks may refer queries about area attractions to a concierge and may direct more complicated questions to the appropriate manager.

In some smaller hotels and motels, where smaller staffs are employed, clerks may take on a variety of additional responsibilities, such as bringing fresh linens to rooms, which usually are performed by employees in other departments of larger lodging establishments. In the smaller places, desk clerks often are responsible for all front-office operations, information and services. For example, they may perform the work of a bookkeeper, advance reservation agent, cashier, laundry attendant and telephone switchboard operator.

Working Conditions: Hotels are open around the clock creating the need for night and weekend work. Extended hours of operation also afford the many part-time job seekers an opportunity to find work in these establishments, especially on evenings and late-night shifts or on weekends and holidays. About half of all desk clerks work a 35 to 40 hour week—most of the rest work fewer hours—so the jobs are attractive to persons seeking part-time work or jobs with flexible schedules. Most clerks work in areas that are clean, well lit and relatively quiet, although lobbies can become crowded and noisy when busy. Many hotels have stringent dress guidelines for desk clerks.

Desk clerks may experience particularly hectic times during check-in and check-out times or incur the pressures encountered when dealing with convention guests or large groups of tourists at one time. Moreover, dealing with irate guests can be stressful. Computer failures can further complicate an already busy time and add to stress levels. Hotel desk clerks may be on their feet most of the time and may occasionally be asked to lift heavy guest luggage.

Training, Other Qualifications and Advancement: Hotel, motel and resort desk clerks deal directly with the public, so a professional appearance and a pleasant personality are important. A clear speaking voice and fluency in English also are essential, because these employees talk directly with hotel guests and the public and frequently use the telephone or public-address systems. Good spelling and computer literacy are needed, because most of the work involves use of a computer. In addition, speaking a foreign language fluently is increasingly helpful, because of the growing international clientele of many properties.

Most hotel, motel and resort desk clerks receive orientation and training on the job. Orientation may include an explanation of the job duties and information about the establishment, such as the arrangement of sleeping rooms, availability of additional services, such as a business or fitness center and location of guest facilities, such as ice and vending machines, restaurants and other nearby retail stores. New employees learn job tasks through on-the-job training under the guidance of a supervisor or an experienced desk clerk. They often receive additional training on interpersonal or customer service skills and on how to use the computerized reservation, room assignment and billing systems and equipment. Desk clerks typically continue to receive instruction on new procedures and on company policies after their initial training ends.

Formal academic training generally is not required so many students take jobs as desk clerks on evening or weekend shifts or during school vacation periods. Most employers look for people who are friendly and customer-service oriented, well groomed and display the maturity and self confidence to demonstrate good judgment. Desk clerks, especially in high-volume and higher-end properties should be quick-thinking, show initiative and be able to work as a member of a team. Hotel managers typically look for these personal characteristics when hiring first-time desk clerks, because it is easier to teach company policy and computer skills than personality traits.

Large hotel and motel chains may offer better opportunities for advancement than small, independently owned establishments. The large chains have more extensive career ladder programmes and may offer desk clerks an opportunity to participate in a management training programme. Also, the Educational Institute of the American Hotel and Motel Association offers home-study or group-study courses in lodging management, which may help some obtain promotions more rapidly.

Employment: Hotel, motel and resort desk clerks held about 195,000 jobs in 2004. Virtually all were in hotels, motels and other establishments in the accommodation industry. Few were self employed.

Job Outlook: Employment of hotel, motel and resort desk clerks is expected to grow about as fast as the average for all occupations through 2014, as more hotels, motels and other lodging establishments are built and occupancy rates rise. Job opportunities for hotel and motel desk clerks also will result from a need to replace workers, because many of these clerks either transfer to other occupations that offer better pay and advancement opportunities or simply leave the workforce altogether. Opportunities for part-time work should continue to be plentiful, because these businesses typically are staffed 24 hours a day, 7 days a week.

Employment of hotel and motel desk clerks should benefit from an increase in business and leisure travel. Shifts in preferences away from long vacations and toward long weekends and other, more frequent, shorter trips also should boost demand for these workers, because such stays increase the number of nights spent in hotels. While many lower budget and extended-stay establishments are being built to cater to families and the leisure traveller, many new luxury and resort accommodations also are opening to serve the upscale client. With the increased number of units requiring staff, employment opportunities for desk clerks should be good.

Growth of hotel, motel and resort desk clerk jobs will be moderated by technology. Automated check-in and check-out procedures reduce the backlog of guests waiting for desk service and may reduce peak front desk staffing needs in many establishments. Nevertheless, the front desk remains the principal point of contact for guests at most properties and most will continue to have clerks on duty.

Employment of desk clerks is sensitive to cyclical swings in the economy. During recessions, vacation and business travel declines and hotels and motels need fewer desk clerks. Similarly, employment is affected by special events, business and convention business and seasonal fluctuations.

Earnings: Median annual earnings of hotel, motel and resort desk clerks were 17,700 in May 2004. The middle 50 percent earned between $15,190 and $21,270. The lowest 10 percent earned less than $13,040, while the highest 10 percent earned more than $25,200.

Earnings of hotel, motel and resort desk clerks vary by a number of seasonal or geographic factors, such as whether the establishment is in a major metropolitan area, a resort community, or other economic or regional characteristic. Earnings also will vary according to the size of the hotel and the level of service offered. For example, luxury hotels that offer guests more personal attention and a greater number of services typically have stricter and more demanding requirements for their desk staff. However, these higher standards of service also result in higher earnings for employees.

Hotel and Motel Managers

Overview: Hotel and motel managers make sure guests receive good service.

As a hotel or motel manager, you have a variety of duties. But for the manager at the Peabody Memphis Hotel in Tennessee, you have one duty that is perhaps a bit out of the ordinary: managing ducks. Since the 1930s, the "March of the Peabody Ducks" has taken place daily at 11 a.m. and 5 p.m. In the morning, a special group of five ducks march from their special "Duck Palace" down a red carpet to the fountain in the hotel's lobby. They hang out there swimming and wading until dinnertime, when the ducks march again on the red carpet back to their palace for the night. The tradition began when two hunters thought it would be funny to put live ducks in the hotel's fountain. The guests thought it was wonderful and the tradition was born.

Although the ducks are led by the Peabody Duck Master, it is still the manager's duty to make sure the Master and the ducks are performing their job duties. (It's not so hard for the ducks, since their job is to splash and swim and live a very pampered life!)

Hotel and motels rent rooms to customers. These businesses need employees to clean rooms and check in guests. Larger hotels also need employees to plan conferences, set up rooms for events and prepare meals for guests. Hotel and motel managers oversee all these departments and make sure employees do good work. Duties vary with the size and type of the business. In small hotels and motels, one manager may be in charge of all departments. In large hotels, each department may be run by an assistant manager. General managers are in charge of the entire hotel. They often help create budgets, policies and advertisements. They also may set room rates and fees.

There are several types of assistant managers. Executive housekeepers are in charge of the workers who clean the hotel. They inspect the hotel to make sure that all areas are clean. Front office managers are in charge of reservations and room assignments. Food and beverage managers oversee restaurants and banquets. They plan menus, set prices and order supplies. Convention services managers coordinate all hotel activities related to meetings. They meet with clients and plan schedules. Then they work with the food service and front office managers to serve and lodge the visitors.

Assistant managers hire, train and supervise the members of their staff. They assign duties to workers and schedule their shifts. They also solve customers' complaints and answer questions about their departments. In addition, managers write reports about their department. They also order food or supplies and may negotiate contracts with vendors. Assistant managers meet and talk with the general manager several times a week. They also talk to other assistant managers when coordinating large events, such as weddings.

In general, managers of small hotels and motels have more duties than managers of larger businesses. This is because there are fewer employees in smaller hotels and motels. Thus, managers are likely to fill in for absent workers. For example, managers may occasionally clean rooms, take reservations, check guests in and out, or make general repairs. Managers of small hotels and motels have many administrative tasks. They interview, hire and train new staff. They schedule laundry service deliveries and order supplies. In addition, they keep track of income and expenses.

Other titles and keywords for this career.

Work Activities: The following list of occupational tasks is specific to this career.

- Coordinate front-office duties. May greet and register guests and show rooms.

- Answer questions about hotel policies and services. Resolve customers' complaints.
- Assign duties to workers and schedule shifts.
- Observe and monitor workers' performance to make sure that procedures are being followed.
- Meet with clients to plan conventions, weddings and banquets.
- Keep track of money earned and spent.
- Confer and cooperate with other managers to coordinate hotel activities, such as weddings.
- Interview, hire and train staff.
- Inspect hotel for cleanliness and appearance.
- Purchase supplies or services, such as laundry, repair and trash, from outside vendors. Negotiate contracts.
- Write reports about department functions. Use computers to keep track of information.
- May set room rates and develop budgets, policies and procedures for hotel operations.
- May design marketing and advertising campaigns.

People in this career perform the following list of tasks, but the tasks are common to many occupations.

- Get information needed to do the job.
- Work with the public.
- Make decisions and solve problems.
- Establish and maintain relationships.
- Document and record information.
- Use computers.
- Communicate with supervisors, peers, or subordinates.
- Resolve conflicts and negotiate with others.
- Convince others to buy goods or change their minds or actions.
- Organize, plan and prioritize work.
- Process information.
- Perform administrative tasks.

- Communicate with people from outside the organization.
- Coordinate the work and activities of others.
- Monitor and control resources.
- Judge the value of objects, services, or people.
- Update and use job-related knowledge.
- Develop goals and strategies.
- Schedule work and activities.
- Evaluate information against standards.

Working Conditions: In a typical work setting, people in this career:

Interpersonal Relationships:

- Have a high level of contact with staff and customers.
- Communicate by telephone and in person on a daily basis. They communicate less often by letters, memos and e-mail.
- Are responsible for the work of the employees they supervise.
- Are sometimes placed in conflict situations with guests who may be angry or unhappy.
- Are responsible for the health and safety of staff and customers.

Physical Work Conditions:

- Often work indoors. Managers at lodges or hotels with gardens or grounds may spend some time outdoors.
- Work near others, usually within a few feet.

Work Performance:

- Must be exact in their work. Managers work hard to make customers feel at home. Any mistakes could cause customers to stay at other hotels in the future.
- Regularly make decisions that have a strong impact on their employer's reputation.
- Make decisions that affect clients and employees on a daily basis. They rarely consult a supervisor before deciding a course of action.

- Set most tasks and goals for the day without consulting a supervisor. Because they are managers, they often direct the tasks and goals of others.
- Work under moderate job pressures. Hotels and motels often compete to attract new customers.
- Abide by weekly deadlines.
- Repeat the same activities, such as meeting customers and operating a computer.

Hours/Travel:

- Generally work a set schedule.
- Most work 40 hours per week. Occasional overtime is common.
- May work evenings and weekends, since hotels are open around the clock.

Physical Demands: People in this career frequently:

- Sit while filling out paperwork and writing reports.
- Stand while supervising events.

It is important for people in this career to be able to:

- Speak clearly so listeners can understand.
- Understand the speech of another person.
- See details of objects that are less than a few feet away.

It is not as important, but still necessary, for people in this career to be able to:

- See details of objects that are more than a few feet away.
- Use stomach and lower back muscles to support the body for long periods without getting tired.
- Move two or more limbs together (for example, two arms, two legs, or one leg and one arm) while remaining in place.

Skills and Abilities: People in this career need to:

Communicate

- Listen to others, understand and ask questions.
- Express ideas clearly when speaking or writing.
- Read and understand written information.

Reason and Problem Solve:

- Analyze ideas and use logic to determine their strengths and weaknesses.
- Understand new information or materials by studying and working with them.
- Judge the costs and benefits of a possible action.
- Notice when something is wrong or is likely to go wrong.
- Use reasoning to discover answers to problems.
- Identify problems and review information. Develop, review and apply solutions.
- Combine several pieces of information and draw conclusions.
- Develop rules or follow guidelines for arranging items.

Use Math and Science:

- Use math skills to solve problems.

Manage Oneself, People, Time and Things:

- Check how well one is learning or doing something.
- Manage the time of self and others.
- Decide how to spend money to get the work done and keep track of how the money was used.
- Motivate, develop and direct people as they work.
- Obtain needed equipment, facilities and materials and oversee their use.

Work with People:

- Be aware of others' reactions and change behaviour in relation to them.
- Look for ways to help people.
- Use several methods to teach others how to do something.
- Solve problems by bringing others together to discuss differences.
- Persuade others to approach things differently.

Work with Things:

- Determine the causes of technical problems and find solutions for them.

Knowledge: People in this career need knowledge in the following areas:

- Customer and Personal Service: Knowledge of providing special services to customers based on their needs.
- Administration and Management: Knowledge of managing the operations of a business, company, or group.
- English Language: Knowledge of the meaning, spelling and use of the English language.
- Sales and Marketing: Knowledge of advertising and selling products and services.
- Personnel and Human Resources: Knowledge of the department that is in charge of the relationship between a company and its employees. In particular, includes knowledge of the activities performed by the department.
- Clerical: Knowledge of general office work such as filing and recording information.
- Economics and Accounting: Knowledge of producing, supplying and using goods and services. Also includes knowledge of the methods for keeping business records.
- Psychology: Knowledge of people, their actions and mental processes. This may include knowledge of how to treat emotional and behavioural problems.
- Mathematics: Knowledge of the rules and uses of numbers. Areas of knowledge include arithmetic, algebra, geometry and statistics.
- Education and Training: Knowledge of teaching and the methods involved in learning and instruction.
- Computers and Electronics: Knowledge of computer hardware and software.
- Public Safety and Security: Knowledge of protecting people, data and property.

Interests: People in this career are people who tend to:

- Consider independence important. They like to make decisions and try out ideas on their own. They prefer jobs where they can plan their work with little supervision.
- Consider good working conditions important. They like

jobs offering steady employment and good pay. They want employment that fits their individual work style. They may prefer doing a variety of tasks, working alone, or being busy all the time.

- Consider relationships important. They like to work in a friendly, non-competitive environment. They like to do things for other people. They prefer jobs where they are not pressured to do things that go against their sense of right and wrong.
- Consider recognition important. They like to work in jobs which have opportunities for them to advance, be recognized for their work and direct and instruct others. They usually prefer jobs in which they are looked up to by others.
- Consider achievement important. They like to see the results of their work and to use their strongest abilities. They like to get a feeling of accomplishment from their work.
- Have enterprising interests. They like work activities that involve starting up and carrying out projects, especially in business. They like to lead and persuade others, make decisions and take risks for profit.
- Have conventional interests. They like work activities that follow set procedures, routines and standards. They like to work with data and detail. They prefer working where there is a clear line of authority to follow.
- Have social interests. They like work activities that assist others and promote learning and personal development. They like to communicate with others: to teach, give advice, help, or otherwise be of service to others.

Preparation: To work as a hotel or motel manager, you must: complete a two-year training programme or work your way up over several years; be self-confident and persuasive; have strong communication skills; and be able to direct and motivate people.

Formal Education: Most hotel and motel managers learn their skills through formal training programmes. Community and junior colleges and some universities offer two- or four-year degree programmes in hotel and motel management. Technical institutes and vocational and trade schools also offer formal programmes. These programmes may be from one to two years long. Most formal programmes include courses in accounting, marketing and food service management.

Employers also hire people who have a degree in another field, such as business or liberal arts.

Work Experience: Some employers promote outstanding employees into management positions. However, this method of advancement is not as common as it once was. You need to boost your experience with some formal training.

Most students, especially those who choose liberal arts degrees, need work experience. An internship or part-time job at a hotel is a good way to gain experience.

On-the-job Training: Larger hotels often provide training. New managers rotate through various departments to learn the business. Other hotels may pay for formal training in hotel management for their outstanding employees. Training may last up to six months.

Outlook: In Minnesota, the number of jobs for hotel and motel managers is expected to grow about as fast as average through the year 2014.

Nationally, the number of jobs for hotel and motel managers is expected to grow as fast as average through the year 2014.

The travel industry is growing again after the lull caused by the events of September 11. Some families and business customers are willing to pay extra for special services. They are willing to pay for suites, which are rooms with kitchens and space to have meetings. Other people prefer to stay at large full-service hotels. These hotels offer fitness centres, large meeting rooms and play areas for children. Both suite and full-service hotels need more managers because of the number of services they provide.

Jobs will be available as workers retire, transfer to other positions, or leave the field. Some people leave the field because of long hours or because of the high amount of contact with customers. Opportunities are very good for people who have a college degree in hotel or restaurant management.

	Employment		*Employment Change*	
	2002	2012	Number	Percent
National	58,200	67,900	9,700	16.7

Advancement Opportunities: Graduates of hotel management programmes usually start as assistant manager trainees. As they gain experience, trainees usually become assistant managers. Eventually they may become general managers.

Larger hotels may offer better opportunities for advancement than smaller hotels. Managers may need to move to hotels in other cities every two years to move up. Certification as a "Certified Rooms Division Specialist" may speed up advancement. See "Licensing/Certification".

Lodging Managers

Significant Points: Long hours, including night and weekend work, are common.

Employment is projected to grow about as fast as the average for all occupations.

College graduates with degrees in hotel or hospitality management should have the best job opportunities.

Nature of the Work: A comfortable room, good food and a helpful staff can make being away from home an enjoyable experience for both vacationing families and business travellers. While most lodging managers work in traditional hotels and motels, some work in other lodging establishments, such as camps, inns, boardinghouses, dude ranches and recreational resorts.

In full-service hotels, lodging managers help their guests have a pleasant stay by providing many of the comforts of home, including cable television, fitness equipment and voice mail, as well as specialized services such as health spas. For business travellers, lodging managers often schedule available meeting rooms and electronic equipment, including slide projectors and fax machines.

Lodging managers are responsible for keeping their establishments efficient and profitable. In a small establishment with a limited staff, the manager may oversee all aspects of operations. However, large hotels may employ hundreds of workers and the general manager usually is aided by a number of assistant managers assigned to the various departments of the operation. In hotels of every size, managerial duties vary significantly by job title.

General managers have overall responsibility for the operation of the hotel. Within guidelines established by the owners of the hotel or executivcs of the hotel chain, the general manager sets room rates, allocates funds to departments, approves expenditures and ensures expected standards for guest service, decor, housekeeping, food quality and banquet operations. Managers who work for chains also may organize and staff a newly built hotel, refurbish an older hotel, or reorganize a hotel or motel that is not operating successfully. In order to fill entry-level service and clerical jobs in hotels, some managers attend career fairs.

Resident or hotel managers are responsible for the day-to-day operations of the property. In larger properties, more than one of these managers may assist the general manager, frequently dividing responsibilities between the food and beverage operations and the rooms or lodging services. At least one manager, either the general manager or a hotel manager, is on call 24 hours a day to resolve problems or emergencies.

Assistant managers help run the day-to-day operations of the hotel. In large hotels, they may be responsible for activities such as personnel, accounting, office administration, marketing and sales, purchasing, security, maintenance and pool, spa, or recreational facilities. In smaller hotels, these duties may be combined into one position. Assistant managers may adjust charges on a hotel guest's bill when a manager is unavailable.

An *Executive Committee* made up of a hotel's senior managers advises the general manager, assists in setting hotel policy, coordinates services that cross departmental boundaries and collaborates on efforts to ensure consistent and efficient guest services throughout the hotel. The Committee may be comprised of the department heads for housekeeping, front office, food and beverage, security, sales and public relations, meetings and conventions, engineering and building maintenance and human resources. Executive committee members bring a different perspective of guest service to the total management objective reflecting the unique expertise and training of their positions.

Executive housekeepers ensure that guest rooms, meeting and banquet rooms and public areas are clean, orderly and well maintained. They also train, schedule and supervise the work of housekeepers, inspect rooms and order cleaning supplies.

Front office managers coordinate reservations and room assignments, as well as train and direct the hotel's front desk staff. They ensure that guests are treated courteously, complaints and problems are resolved and requests for special services are carried out. Front office managers may adjust charges posted on a customer's bill.

Convention services managers coordinate the activities of various departments in larger hotels to accommodate meetings, conventions and special events. They meet with representatives of groups or organizations to plan the number of rooms to reserve, the desired configuration of the meeting space and banquet services. During the meeting or event, they resolve unexpected problems and monitor activities to ensure that hotel operations conform to the expectations of the group.

Food and beverage managers oversee all food service operations maintained by the hotel. They coordinate menus with the Executive Chef for the hotel's restaurants, lounges and room service operations. They supervise the ordering of food and supplies, direct service and maintenance contracts within the kitchens and dining areas and manage food service budgets.

Catering managers arrange for food service in a hotel's meeting and convention rooms. They coordinate menus and costs for banquets, parties and events with meeting and convention planners or individual clients. They coordinate staffing needs and arrange schedules with kitchen personnel to ensure appropriate food service.

Sales or marketing directors and *public relations directors* oversee the advertising and promotion of hotel operations and functions, including lodging and dining specials and special events, such as holiday or seasonal specials. They direct the efforts of their staff to purchase advertising and market their property to organizations or groups seeking a venue for conferences, conventions, business meetings, trade shows and special events. They also coordinate media relations and answer questions from the press.

Human resources directors manage the personnel functions of a hotel, ensuring that all accounting, payroll and employee relations matters are handled in compliance with hotel policy and applicable laws. They also oversee hiring practices and standards and ensure that training and promotion programmes reflect appropriate employee development guidelines.

Finance (or revenue) directors monitor room sales and reservations. In addition to overseeing accounting and cash-flow matters at the hotel, they also project occupancy levels, decide which rooms to discount and when to offer rate specials.

Computers are used extensively by lodging managers and their assistants to keep track of guests' bills, reservations, room assignments, meetings and special events. In addition, computers are used to order food, beverages and supplies, as well as to prepare reports for hotel owners and top-level managers. Managers work with computer specialists to ensure that the hotel's computer system functions properly. Should the hotel's computer system fail, managers must continue to meet the needs of hotel guests and staff.

Working Conditions: Because hotels are open around the clock, night and weekend work is common. Many lodging managers work more than 40 hours per week and may be called back to work at any time. Some managers of resort properties or other hotels where much of the business is seasonal have other duties on the property during the off-season or find work at other hotels or in other areas.

Lodging managers experience the pressures of coordinating a wide range of activities. At larger hotels, they also carry the burden of managing a large staff and finding a way to satisfy guest needs while maintaining positive attitudes and employee morale. Conventions and large groups of tourists may present unusual problems or require extended work hours. Moreover, dealing with irate guests can be stressful. The job can be particularly hectic for front office managers during check-in and check-out times. Computer failures can further complicate processing and add to frustration levels.

Training, Other Qualifications and Advancement: Hotels increasingly emphasize specialized training. Postsecondary training in hotel, restaurant, or hospitality management is preferred for most hotel management positions; however, a college liberal arts degree may be sufficient when coupled with related hotel experience or business education. Internships or part-time or summer work experience in a hotel are an asset to students seeking a career in hotel management. The experience gained and the contacts made with employers can greatly benefit students after graduation. Most degree programmes include work-study opportunities.

Community colleges, junior colleges and many universities offer certificate or degree programmes in hotel, restaurant, or hospitality management leading to an associate, bachelor, or graduate degree. Technical institutes, vocational and trade schools and other academic institutions also offer courses leading to formal recognition in hospitality management. In total, more than 800 educational facilities provide academic training for would-be lodging managers. Hotel management programmes include instruction in hotel administration, accounting, economics, marketing, housekeeping, food service management and catering and hotel maintenance engineering. Computer training also is an integral part of hotel management training, due to the widespread use of computers in reservations, billing and housekeeping management.

More than 450 high schools in 45 States offer the Lodging Management Programme created by the Educational Institute of the American Hotel and Lodging Association. This two-year programme offered to high school juniors and seniors teaches management principles and leads to a professional certification called the "Certified Rooms Division Specialist." Many colleges and universities grant participants credit towards a post-secondary degree in hotel management.

Lodging managers must be able to get along with many different types of people, even in stressful situations. They must be able to solve problems and concentrate on details. Initiative, self-discipline, effective communication skills and the ability to organize and direct the work of others also are essential for managers at all levels.

Persons wishing to make a career in the hospitality industry may be promoted into a management trainee position sponsored by the hotel or a hotel chain's corporate parent. Typically, trainees work as assistant managers and may rotate assignments among the hotel's departments—front office, housekeeping, or food and beverage—to gain a wide range of experiences. Relocation to another property may be required to help round out the experience and to help grow a trainee into the position.

Work experience in the hospitality industry at any level or in any segment, including summer jobs or part-time work in a hotel or restaurant, is good background for entering hotel management. Most employers require a bachelor's degree with some education in business and computer literacy, while some prefer a master's degree for hotel management positions. However, employees who demonstrate leadership potential and possess sufficient length or breadth of experience may be invited to participate in a management training programme and advance to hotel management positions without the education beyond high school.

Large hotel and motel chains may offer better opportunities for advancement than small, independently owned establishments, but relocation every several years often is necessary for advancement. The large chains have more extensive career ladder programmes and offer managers the opportunity to transfer to another hotel or motel in the chain or to the central office. Career advancement can be accelerated by the completion of certification programmes offered by various associations. These programmes usually require a combination of course work, examinations and experience. For example, outstanding lodging managers may advance to higher level manager positions.

Employment: Lodging managers held about 58,000 jobs in 2004. Self-employed managers—primarily owners of small hotels, motels and inns—held about 45 percent of these jobs. Companies that manage hotels and motels under contract employed many managers.

Job Outlook: Employment of lodging managers is expected to grow about as fast as the average for all occupations through 2014. Additional job openings are expected to occur as experienced managers transfer to other occupations or leave the labour force, in part because of the long hours and stressful working conditions. Job opportunities are expected to be best for persons with college degrees in hotel or hospitality management.

Renewed business travel and domestic and foreign tourism will drive employment growth of lodging managers in full-service hotels. The numbers of economy-class rooms and extended-stay hotels also are expected to increase to accommodate leisure travellers and bargain-conscious guests. An increasing range of lodging accommodations is available to travellers, from economy hotels which offer clean, comfortable rooms and front desk services without costly extras such as restaurants and room service, to luxury and boutique inns that offer sumptuous furnishings and personal services. The accommodation industry is expected to continue to consolidate as lodging chains acquire independently owned establishments or undertake their operation on a contract basis. The increasing number of extended-stay hotels will moderate growth of manager jobs because these properties usually have fewer departments and require fewer managers. Also, these establishments often do not require a manager to be available 24 hours a day, instead assigning front desk clerks on duty at night some of the responsibilities previously reserved for managers.

Additional demand for managers is expected in suite hotels, because some guests—especially business customers—are willing to pay higher prices for rooms with kitchens and suites that provide the space needed to conduct small meetings. In addition, large full-service hotels—offering restaurants, fitness centres, large meeting rooms and play areas for children, among other amenities—will continue to provide many trainee and managerial opportunities.

Earnings: Median annual earnings of lodging managers were $37,660 in May 2004. The middle 50 percent earned between $28,640 and $51,030. The lowest 10 percent earned less than $22,680, while the highest 10 percent earned more than $72,160. Median annual earnings for lodging managers in traveller accommodations were $37,420.

Salaries of lodging managers vary greatly according to their responsibilities and the segment of the hotel industry in which they are employed, as well as the location and region where the hotel is located. Managers may earn bonuses of up to 25 percent of their basic salary in some hotels and also may be furnished with meals, parking, laundry and other services. In addition to providing typical benefits, some hotels offer profit-sharing plans and educational assistance to their employees.

Hotel Managers and Assistants

Significant Points:

- Long hours and the stress of dealing with hotel patrons result in high turnover among hotel managers.
- College graduates with degrees in hotel or restaurant management should have good job opportunities.

Nature of the Work: A comfortable room, good food and a helpful hotel staff can make being away from home an enjoyable experience for both vacationing families and business travellers. Hotel managers and assistant managers help their guests have a pleasant stay by providing many of the comforts of home, including cable television, fitness equipment and voice mail. Additionally, some hotels have health spas and other specialized services that the hotel manager and assistant help keep running smoothly. For business travellers, hotel managers often schedule available meeting rooms and electronic equipment, including slide projectors and fax machines.

Hotel managers are responsible for keeping the operation of their establishments efficient and profitable. In a small hotel, motel, or inn with a limited staff, the manager may oversee all aspects of operations. However, large hotels may employ hundreds of workers and the general manager is usually aided by a number of assistant managers assigned to the various departments of the operation. In hotels of every size, managerial duties vary significantly by job title.

The general manager, for example, has overall responsibility for the operation of the hotel. Within guidelines established by the owners of the hotel or executives of the hotel chain, the general manager sets room rates, allocates funds to departments, approves expenditures and establishes standards for service to guests, decor, housekeeping, food quality and banquet operations. Managers who work for chains may also organize and staff a newly built hotel, refurbish an older hotel, or reorganize a hotel or motel that is not operating successfully. In order to fill some low-paying service and clerical jobs in hotels, some general managers attend career fairs.

Resident managers live in hotels and are on call 24 hours a day to resolve problems or emergencies. In general, though, they typically work an 8-hour day and oversee the day-to-day operations of the hotel. In many hotels, the general manager is also the resident manager.

Executive housekeepers ensure guest rooms, meeting and banquet rooms and public areas are clean, orderly and well maintained. They also train, schedule and supervise the work of housekeepers, inspect rooms and order cleaning supplies.

Front office managers coordinate reservations and room assignments as well as train and direct the hotel's front desk staff. They ensure that guests are treated courteously, complaints and problems are resolved and requests for special services are carried out. Front office managers often have authorization to adjust charges posted on a customer's bill.

Food and beverage managers direct the food service operations of hotels. They oversee the hotels' restaurants, cocktail lounges and banquet facilities. These managers also supervise food and beverage preparation and service workers, plan menus, set schedules, estimate costs and deal with food suppliers.

Convention services managers coordinate the activities of large hotels' various departments for meetings, conventions and special events. They meet with representatives of groups or organizations to plan the number of rooms to reserve, the desired configuration of hotel meeting space and the banquet services. During the meeting or event, they resolve unexpected problems and monitor activities to ensure that hotel operations conform to the expectations of the group.

Assistant managers help run the day-to-day operations of the hotel. In large hotels they may be responsible for activities such as personnel, accounting, office administration, marketing and sales, purchasing, security, maintenance and pool, spa, or recreational facilities. In smaller hotels, these duties may be combined into one position. Some hotels allow an assistant manager to make decisions regarding hotel guest charges when a manager is unavailable.

Computers are used extensively by hotel managers and their assistants to keep track of the guest's bill, reservations, room assignments, meetings and special events. In addition, computers are used to order food, beverages and supplies, as well as to prepare reports for hotel owners and top-level managers. Managers work with computer specialists to ensure that the hotel's computer system functions properly. Should the hotel's computer system fail, managers must continue to meet guests' needs.

Working Conditions: Because hotels are open around the clock, night and weekend work is common. Many hotel managers work more than 40 hours per week. Managers who live in the hotel usually have regular work schedules, but they may be called to work at any time. Some employees of resort hotels are managers during the busy season and have other duties during the rest of the year.

Hotel managers sometimes experience the pressures of coordinating a wide range of functions. Conventions and large groups of tourists may present unusual problems. Moreover, dealing with irate guests can be stressful. The job can be particularly hectic for front office managers during check-in and check-out time. Computer failures can further complicate an already busy time.

Employment: Hotel managers and assistant managers held about 76,000 jobs in 1998. Self-employed managers-primarily owners of small hotels and motels-held a significant number of these jobs. Companies that manage hotels and motels under contract employed some managers.

Training, Other Qualifications and Advancement: Hotels increasingly emphasize specialized training. Postsecondary training in hotel or restaurant management is preferred for most hotel management positions, although a college liberal arts degree may be sufficient when coupled with related hotel experience. Internships or part-time or summer work is an asset to students seeking a career in hotel management. The experience gained and the contacts made with employers can greatly benefit them after graduation. Most bachelor's degree programmes include work-study opportunities.

In the past, many managers were promoted from the ranks of front desk clerks, housekeepers, waiters and chefs and hotel sales workers. Although some employees still advance to hotel management positions without education beyond high school, postsecondary education is preferred. Restaurant management training or experience is also a good background for entering hotel management because the success of a hotel's food service and beverage operations is often of great importance to the profitability of the entire establishment.

In 1998, nearly 200 community and junior colleges and some universities offered associate, bachelor's and graduate degree programmes in hotel or restaurant management. When combined with technical institutes, vocational and trade schools and other academic institutions, over 800 educational facilities have programmes leading to formal recognition in hotel or restaurant management. Hotel management programmes include instruction in hotel administration, accounting, economics, marketing, housekeeping, food service management and catering and hotel maintenance engineering. Computer training is also an integral part of hotel management training due to the widespread use of computers in reservations, billing and housekeeping management.

Hotel managers must be able to get along with many different people, even in stressful situations. They must be able to solve problems and concentrate on details. Initiative, self-discipline, effective communication skills and the ability to organize and direct the work of others are also essential for managers at all levels.

Most hotels promote employees who have proven their ability and completed formal education in hotel management. Graduates of hotel or restaurant management programmes usually start as trainee assistant managers. Some large hotels sponsor specialized on-the-job management training programmes allowing trainees to rotate among various departments and gain a thorough knowledge of the hotel's operation. Other hotels may help finance formal training in hotel management for outstanding employees. Newly built hotels, particularly those without well-established on-the-job training programmes, often prefer experienced personnel for managerial positions.

Large hotel and motel chains may offer better opportunities for advancement than small, independently owned establishments, but relocation every several years often is necessary for advancement. The large chains have more extensive career ladder programmes and offer managers the opportunity to transfer to another hotel or motel in the chain or to the central office. Career advancement can be accelerated by completion of certification programmes offered by the associations listed below. These programmes usually require a combination of course work, examinations and experience.

Job Outlook: Employment of hotel managers and assistants is expected to grow more slowly than the average for all occupations through 2008. Long hours and stressful working conditions result in high turnover in this field, so additional job openings are expected to occur as experienced managers transfer to other occupations, retire, or stop working for other reasons. Job opportunities in hotel management are expected to be especially good for persons with college degrees in hotel or restaurant management.

Increasing business travel and domestic and foreign tourism will drive employment growth of hotel managers and assistants. Managerial jobs are not expected to grow as rapidly as the hotel industry overall, however. As the industry consolidates, many chains and franchises will acquire independently owned establishments and increase the number of economy-class rooms to accommodate bargain-conscious guests. Economy hotels offer clean, comfortable rooms and front desk services without costly extras like restaurants and room service. Because there are not as many departments in these hotels, fewer managers will be needed. In addition, front desk clerks are increasingly assuming some responsibilities previously reserved for managers, further limiting the growth of managers and their assistants.

Additional demand for managers, however, is expected in suite hotels as some guests, especially business customers, are willing to pay higher prices for rooms with kitchens and suites that provide the space needed to conduct meetings. In addition to job growth in suite hotels and economy-class hotels, large full-service hotels-offering restaurants, fitness centres, large meeting rooms and play areas for children, among other amenities-will continue to offer many trainee and managerial opportunities.

Earnings: Median annual earnings of hotel managers and assistants were $26,700 in 1998. The middle 50 percent of these workers earned between $19,820 and $34,690. The lowest 10 percent had earnings of less than $14,430, while the top 10 percent earned over $45,520. In 1997, median annual earnings in the hotel and other lodging places industry, where nearly all of these workers are employed, were $28,600.

Salaries of hotel managers and assistants vary greatly according to their responsibilities and the segment of the hotel industry in which they are employed. Managers may earn bonuses up to 25 percent of their basic salary in some hotels and may also be furnished with lodging, meals, parking, laundry and other services. In addition to typical benefits, some hotels offer profit-sharing plans and educational assistance to their employees.

Related Occupations: Other occupations concerned with organizing and directing a business where customer service is the cornerstone of their success include restaurant managers, apartment building managers, retail store managers and office managers.

Food and Beverage Serving and Related Workers

Significant Points: Most jobs are part time so many opportunities exist for young people—about one-fourth of these workers were 16 to 19 years old, almost six times the proportion for all workers.

Job openings are expected to be abundant through 2014 because many of these workers transfer to other occupations or stop working, creating numerous openings.

Tips comprise a major portion of earnings, so keen competition is expected for jobs where potential earnings from tips are greatest—bartenders, waiters and waitresses and other jobs in popular restaurants and fine dining establishments.

Nature of the Work: Food and beverage serving and related workers are the front line of customer service in restaurants, coffee shops and other food service establishments. These workers greet customers, escort them to seats and hand them menus, take food and drink orders and serve food and beverages. They also answer questions, explain menu items and specials and keep tables and dining areas clean and set for new diners. Most work as part of a team, helping coworkers to improve workflow and customer service.

Waiters and waitresses, the largest group of these workers, take customers' orders, serve food and beverages, prepare itemized checks and sometimes accept payment. Their specific duties vary considerably, depending on the establishment. In coffee shops serving routine, straightforward fare, such as salads, soups and sandwiches, servers are expected to provide fast, efficient and courteous service. In fine dining restaurants, where more complicated meals are prepared and often served over several courses, waiters and waitresses provide more formal service emphasizing personal, attentive treatment and a more leisurely pace. They may recommend certain dishes and identify ingredients or explain how various items on the menu are prepared. Some prepare salads, desserts, or other menu items tableside. Additionally, they may check the identification of patrons to ensure they meet the minimum age requirement for the purchase of alcohol and tobacco products.

Waiters and waitresses sometimes perform the duties of other food and beverage service workers. These tasks may include escorting guests to tables, serving customers seated at counters, clearing and setting up tables, or operating a cash register. However, full-service restaurants frequently hire other staff, such as hosts and hostesses, cashiers, or dining room attendants, to perform these duties.

Bartenders fill drink orders either taken directly from patrons at the bar or through waiters and waitresses who place drink orders for dining room customers. Bartenders check identification of customers seated at the bar, to ensure they meet the minimum age requirement for the purchase of alcohol and tobacco products. They prepare mixed drinks, serve bottled or draught beer and pour wine or other beverages. Bartenders must know a wide range of drink recipes and be able to mix drinks accurately, quickly and without waste. Besides mixing and serving drinks, bartenders stock and prepare garnishes for drinks; maintain an adequate supply of ice, glasses and other bar supplies; and keep the bar area clean for customers. They also may collect payment, operate the cash register, wash glassware and utensils and serve food to customers seated at the bar. Bartenders usually are responsible for ordering and maintaining an inventory of liquor, mixes and other bar supplies.

The majority of bartenders directly serve and interact with patrons. Bartenders should be friendly and enjoy talking with customers. Bartenders at service bars, on the other hand, have less contact with customers. They work in small bars often located off the kitchen in restaurants, hotels and clubs where only waiters and waitresses place drink orders. Some establishments, especially larger, higher volume ones, use equipment that automatically measures, pours and mixes drinks at the push of a button. Bartenders who use this equipment, however, still must work quickly to handle a large volume of drink orders and be familiar with the ingredients for special drink requests. Much of a bartender's work still must be done by hand to fill each individual order.

Hosts and hostesses welcome guests and maintain reservation or waiting lists. They may direct patrons to coatrooms, restrooms, or to a place to wait until their table is ready. Hosts and hostesses assign guests to tables suitable for the size of their group, escort patrons to their seats and provide menus. They also schedule dining reservations, arrange parties and organize any special services that are required. In some restaurants, they act as cashiers.

Dining room and cafeteria attendants and bartender helpers assist waiters, waitresses and bartenders by cleaning tables, removing dirty dishes and keeping serving areas stocked with supplies. Sometimes called backwaiters or runners, they bring meals out of the kitchen and assist waiters and waitresses by distributing dishes to individual diners. They also replenish the supply of clean linens, dishes, silverware and glasses in the dining room and keep the bar stocked with glasses, liquor, ice and drink garnishes. Dining room attendants set tables with clean tablecloths, napkins, silverware, glasses and dishes and serve ice water, rolls and butter. At the conclusion of meals, they remove dirty dishes and soiled linens from tables. Cafeteria attendants stock serving tables with food, trays, dishes and silverware and may carry trays to dining tables for patrons. *Bartender helpers* keep bar equipment clean and wash glasses. *Dishwashers* clean dishes, cutlery and kitchen utensils and equipment.

Counter attendants take orders and serve food in cafeterias, coffee shops and carryout eateries. In cafeterias, they serve food displayed on steam tables, carve meat, dish out vegetables, ladle sauces and soups and fill beverage glasses. In lunchrooms and coffee shops, counter attendants take orders from customers seated at the counter, transmit orders to the kitchen and pick up and serve food. They also fill cups with coffee, soda and other beverages and prepare fountain specialties, such as milkshakes and ice cream sundaes. Counter attendants also take carryout orders from diners and wrap or place items in containers. They clean counters, write itemized checks and sometimes accept payment. Some counter attendants may prepare short-order items, such as sandwiches and salads.

Some food and beverage serving workers take orders from customers at counters or drive-through windows at fast-food restaurants. They assemble orders, hand them to customers and accept payment. Many of these are *combined food preparation and serving workers* who also cook and package food, make coffee and fill beverage cups using drink-dispensing machines.

Other workers serve food to patrons outside of a restaurant environment, such as in hotels, hospital rooms, or cars.

Working Conditions: Food and beverage service workers are on their feet most of the time and often carry heavy trays of food, dishes and glassware. During busy dining periods, they are under pressure to serve customers quickly and efficiently. The work is relatively safe, but care must be taken to avoid slips, falls and burns.

Part-time work is more common among food and beverage serving and related workers than among workers in almost any other occupation. In 2004, those on part-time schedules included half of all waiters and waitresses and 40 percent of all bartenders.

Food service and drinking establishments typically maintain long dining hours and offer flexible and varied work opportunities. Many food and beverage serving and related workers work evenings, weekends and holidays. Many students and teenagers seek part time or seasonal work as food and beverage serving and related workers as a first job to gain work experience or to earn spending money while in school. Around one-fourth of food and beverage serving and related workers were 16 to 19 years old—about six times the proportion for all workers.

Training, Other Qualifications and Advancement: There are no specific educational requirements for food and beverage service jobs. Many employers prefer to hire high school graduates for waiter and waitress, bartender and host and hostess positions, but completion of high school usually is not required for fast-food workers, counter attendants, dishwashers and dining room attendants and bartender helpers. For many people a job as a food and beverage service worker serves as a source of immediate income, rather than a career. Many entrants to these jobs are in their late teens or early twenties and have a high school education or less. Usually, they have little or no work experience. Many are full-time students or homemakers. Food and beverage service jobs are a major source of part-time employment for high school and college students.

Restaurants rely on good food and quality customer service to retain loyal customers and succeed in a competitive industry. Food and beverage serving and related workers who exhibit excellent personal qualities—such as a neat clean appearance, a well-spoken manner, an ability to work as a member of team and a pleasant way with patrons—will be highly sought after.

Waiters and waitresses need a good memory to avoid confusing customers' orders and to recall faces, names and preferences of frequent patrons. These workers also should be comfortable using computers to place orders and generate customers' bills. Some may need to be quick at arithmetic so they can total bills manually. Knowledge of a foreign language is helpful to communicate with a diverse clientele and staff. Prior experience waiting on tables is preferred by restaurants and hotels that have rigid table service standards. Jobs at these establishments often offer higher wages and have greater income potential from tips, but they may also have stiffer employment requirements than other establishments, such as prior table service experience or higher education.

Usually, bartenders must be at least 21 years of age, but employers prefer to hire people who are 25 or older. Bartenders should be familiar with State and local laws concerning the sale of alcoholic beverages.

Most food and beverage serving and related workers pick up their skills on the job by observing and working with more experienced workers. Some full-service restaurants also provide new dining room employees with some form of classroom-type training that alternates with periods of actual on-the-job work experience. These training programmes communicate the operating philosophy of the restaurant, help establish a personal rapport with other staff and instill a desire to work as a team. They also provide an opportunity to discuss customer service situations and the proper ways of handling unpleasant circumstances or unruly patrons with new employees. Additionally, managers, chefs and servers may meet before each shift to discuss the menu and any new items or specials, review ingredients for any potential food allergies, or talk about any food safety concerns, coordination between the kitchen and the dining room, or any customer service issues from the previous day or shift.

Some employers, particularly those in fast-food restaurants, use self-instruction or online programmes with audiovisual presentations and instructional booklets to teach new employees food preparation and service skills. Some public and private vocational schools, restaurant associations and large restaurant chains provide classroom training in a generalized food service curriculum. All employees receive training on safe food handling procedures and sanitation practices.

Some bartenders acquire their skills by attending a bartending or vocational and technical school. These programmes often include instruction on State and local laws and regulations, cocktail recipes, proper attire and conduct and stocking a bar. Some of these schools help their graduates find jobs. Although few employers require any minimum level of educational attainment, some specialized training is usually needed in food handling and legal issues surrounding serving alcoholic beverages and tobacco. Employers are more likely to hire and promote based on people skills and personal qualities rather than education.

Due to the relatively small size of most food-serving establishments, opportunities for promotion are limited. After gaining experience, some dining room and cafeteria attendants and bartender helpers advance to waiter, waitress, or bartender jobs. For waiters, waitresses and bartenders, advancement usually is limited to finding a job in a busier or more expensive restaurant or bar where prospects for tip earnings are better. Some bartenders, hosts and hostesses and waiters and waitresses advance to supervisory jobs, such as dining room supervisor, maitre d'hotel, assistant manager, or restaurant general manager. A few bartenders open their own businesses. In larger restaurant chains, food and beverage service workers who excel at their work often are invited to enter the company's formal management training programme.

Employment: Food and beverage serving and related workers held 6.8 million jobs in 2004. The distribution of jobs among the various food and beverage serving workers was as follows:

Waiters and waitresses	2,252,000
Combined food preparation and serving workers, including fast food	2,150,000
Dishwashers	507,000
Bartenders	474,000
Counter attendants, cafeteria, food concession and coffee shop	465,000
Dining room and cafeteria attendants and bartender helpers	401,000
Hosts and hostesses, restaurant, lounge and coffee shop	328,000
Food servers, nonrestaurant	189,000
All other food preparation and serving related workers	64,000

The overwhelming majority of jobs for food and beverage serving and related workers were found in food services and drinking places, such as restaurants, coffee shops and bars. Other jobs were found primarily in traveller accommodation (hotels); amusement, gambling and recreation industries; educational services; grocery stores; nursing care facilities; civic and social organizations; and hospitals.

Jobs are located throughout the country but are typically plentiful in large cities and tourist areas. Vacation resorts offer seasonal employment and some workers alternate between summer and winter resorts, instead of remaining in one area the entire year.

Job Outlook: Job openings are expected to be abundant for food and beverage serving and related workers. Overall employment of these workers is expected to increase as fast as the average over the 2004-14 period as population, personal incomes and employment expand. While employment growth will create many new jobs, the overwhelming majority of openings will arise from the need to replace the high proportion of workers who leave the occupations each year. There is substantial movement into and out of these occupations because education and training requirements are minimal and the predominance of part-time jobs are attractive to people seeking a short-term source of income rather than a career. However, keen competition is expected for bartender, waiter and waitress and other food and beverage service jobs in popular restaurants and fine dining establishments, where potential earnings from tips are greatest.

Projected employment growth between 2004 and 2014 varies somewhat by type of job; however, average employment growth is expected for almost all food and beverage serving and related occupations. Employment of combined food preparation and serving workers, which includes fast-food workers, is expected to increase as fast as the average in response to the continuing fast-paced lifestyle of many Americans and the addition of healthier foods at many fast-food restaurants.

Average employment growth is expected for waiters and waitresses and hosts and hostesses because increases in the number of families and the more affluent, 55-and-older population will result in more restaurants that offer table service and more varied menus. Employment of bartenders, dining room attendants and dishwashers will grow more slowly than other food and beverage serving and related workers because diners increasingly are eating at more casual dining spots, such as coffee bars and sandwich shops, rather than at the full-service restaurants and drinking places that employ more of these workers.

Earnings: Food and beverage serving and related workers derive their earnings from a combination of hourly wages and customer tips. Earnings vary greatly, depending on the type of job and establishment. For example, fast-food workers and hosts and hostesses usually do not receive tips, so their wage rates may be higher than those of waiters and waitresses and bartenders in full-service restaurants, who typically earn more from tips than from wages. In some restaurants, workers contribute all or a portion of their tips to a tip pool, which is distributed among qualifying workers. Tip pools allow workers who don't usually receive tips directly from customers, such as dining room attendants, to feel a part of a team and to share in the rewards of good service.

In May 2004, median hourly earnings (including tips) of waiters and waitresses were $6.75. The middle 50 percent earned between $6.04 and $8.34. The lowest 10 percent earned less than $5.60 and the highest 10 percent earned more than $11.27 an hour. For most waiters and waitresses, higher earnings are primarily the result of receiving more in tips rather than higher hourly wages. Tips usually average between 10 and 20 percent of guests' checks; waiters and waitresses working in busy, expensive restaurants earn the most.

Bartenders had median hourly earnings (including tips) of $7.42 in May 2004. The middle 50 percent earned between $6.34 and $9.26. The lowest 10 percent earned less than $5.72 and the highest 10 percent earned more than $12.47 an hour. Like waiters and waitresses, bartenders employed in public bars may receive more than half of their earnings as tips. Service bartenders often are paid higher hourly wages to offset their lower tip earnings.

Median hourly earnings (including tips) of dining room and cafeteria attendants and bartender helpers were $7.10 in May 2004. The middle 50 percent earned between $6.24 and $8.25. The lowest 10 percent earned less than $5.68 and the highest 10 percent earned more than $9.88 an hour. Most received over half of their earnings as wages; the rest of their income was a share of the proceeds from tip pools.

Median hourly earnings of hosts and hostesses were $7.52 in May 2004. The middle 50 percent earned between $6.48 and $8.63. The lowest 10 percent earned less than $5.77 and the highest 10 percent earned more than $10.49 an hour. Wages comprised the majority of their earnings. In some cases, wages were supplemented by proceeds from tip pools.

Median hourly earnings of combined food preparation and serving workers, including fast food, were $7.06 in May 2004. The middle 50 percent earned between $6.18 and $8.25. The lowest 10 percent earned less than $5.65 and the highest 10 percent earned more than $9.85 an hour. Although some combined food preparation and serving workers receive a part of their earnings as tips, fast-food workers usually do not.

Median hourly earnings of counter attendants in cafeterias, food concessions and coffee shops (including tips) were $7.53 in May 2004. The middle 50 percent earned between $6.50 and $8.59 an hour. The lowest 10 percent earned less than $5.80 and the highest 10 percent earned more than $10.38 an hour.

Median hourly earnings of dishwashers were $7.35 in May 2004. The middle 50 percent earned between $6.41 and $8.37. The lowest 10 percent earned less than $5.76 and the highest 10 percent earned more than $9.81 an hour.

Median hourly earnings of nonrestaurant food servers were $7.95 in May 2004. The middle 50 percent earned between $6.64 and $9.98. The lowest 10 percent earned less than $5.86 and the highest 10 percent earned more than $12.53 an hour.

Many beginning or inexperienced workers start earning the Federal minimum wage of $5.15 an hour. However, a few States set minimum wages higher than the Federal minimum. Also, various minimum wage exceptions apply under specific circumstances to disabled workers, full-time students, youth under age 20 in their first 90 days of employment, tipped employees and student-learners. Tipped employees are those who customarily and regularly receive more than $30 a month in tips. The employer may consider tips as part of wages, but the employer must pay at least $2.13 an hour in direct wages. Employers also are permitted to deduct from wages the cost, or fair value, of any meals or lodging provided. Many employers, however, provide free meals and furnish uniforms. Food and beverage service workers who work full time often receive typical benefits, while part-time workers usually do not.

In some large restaurants and hotels, food and beverage serving and related workers belong to unions—principally the

Hotel Employees and Restaurant Employees International Union and the Service Employees International Union.

Catering Manager

Although the job title does not have a specific definition, catering managers mostly work for outside catering firms, business or factory canteens, hospitals or schools. Their job can include hiring, training and motivating staff, organising staff rotas, overseeing the budget and ordering supplies for forthcoming menus. The most important part of the job is achieving good quality at low cost and maintaining high standards of hygiene and customer satisfaction. Catering managers do this by keeping a constant eye on the standard of the ingredients, the meals, the restaurant environment and the service.

Entry Level: Some restaurant and catering managers start as waiters or waitresses, chefs or cooks, counter service assistants or kitchen assistants. For these jobs, no formal qualifications are necessary, although some employers might expect you to have some GCSEs/S grades (A-E/1-5), especially in English and maths. In Scotland, anyone handling food needs an elementary food hygiene certificate.

A one- or two-year full-time college qualification in catering and hospitality can be a good start and a second language could prove useful. Many hotels and restaurant chains run management training schemes. You may be able to join straight from school A levels/H grades, but most employers ask for further or higher educational qualifications such as a BTEC/SQA national certificate/diploma, HNC/HND or a degree.

Making the Grade: Most entry-level positions are at supervisory or assistant manager level. Ideally, you should aim for a first post that offers good all-round experience as well as a training programmeme, which will stand you in good stead as you progress within the industry.

Previous relevant work experience is often a requirement and this type of employment is usually easy to find. Most people who enter the profession have started out by doing part-time or seasonal work in catering outlets such as pubs, restaurants and fast food outlets at weekends and during university holidays.

While working, you may study part time for NVQs/SVQs, or for the Hotel and Catering International Management Association (HCIMA) Advanced Certificate in Hospitality Studies. To study for this, you would need at least two years' relevant experience and must be working at supervisory level in the industry. Management training is likely to include specialised courses in subjects such as finance, marketing, human resources, food safety and training.

With around a third of restaurants owned by groups, there is scope for promotion, which could lead to the management of a regional area for a chain of hotels or restaurants. There are also opportunities to move into hotel or leisure management.

Personal Qualities: As a catering manager, you would need to be a good motivator and leader, good at thinking quickly and sorting out problems on the spot and able to stay calm in a crisis.

You must have an appreciation of customer expectations and commercial demands, the stamina to work long hours and the ability to work under stress.

A smart personal appearance would be essential, together with good communication skills and the flexibility to cope with fraying tempers in a hot kitchen.

Looking Ahead: An increasing number of catering managers are needed for jobs in business and industry, schools and colleges, the health service and the armed forces. With the right experience behind them, many catering managers start their own contract catering businesses.

There is a concentration of catering management opportunities in London and the south east of England, but there is no shortage of potential work in towns and cities throughout the UK.

Alternative Suggestions: Other possibilities might include training as a chef, hotel manager or leisure services manager. The Hospitality and Catering or Leisure and Tourism industries present Global Opportunities.

Take-home Pay: A junior restaurant or catering manger could earn between £13,500 and £18,000.

With experience, a manager's salary could rise to between £17,000 and £27,000.

A senior manager could earn £40,000 or more.

Effects: Working in catering management often involves shift work and unsocial and long hours, which can impact on your personal life. There are, however, catering service operations within business, industry and institutions, in which you would be more likely to work normal office hours.

If you are managing a restaurant, the job usually involves working in the evenings - often staying until after the restaurant is closed - and at weekends and public holidays. Your time off would usually be organised on a shift system.

Chef: Chefs prepare food in the kitchen of a restaurant or for outside catering. Large kitchens in hotels or restaurants are split into different sections for different stages of preparing meals, with a team to prepare and cook the vegetables, for example, another for pastries and breads and so on. New entrants usually start their training as commis chefs (junior or apprentice chefs), learning about each of the different sections, how to cook meat and fish and how to make sauces and desserts. They also learn how to use kitchen equipment safely - from sharp knives to professional mixers - and may have to wash up and look after the kitchen utensils.

They should progress to take responsibility for one of the sections, becoming a chef de partie, answerable to the sous chef, or under-chef. The head chef, also called executive chef or chef de cuisine, is in charge of the whole kitchen, the quality of the food and the teams of chefs. Head chefs have to plan the menu, order supplies of ingredients, manage the budget and keep the kitchen running efficiently. In smaller restaurants, head chefs prepare and cook the food themselves, perhaps with the help of a few assistants.

Entry Level: Many chefs start without any formal qualifications and learn their skills in the kitchen, although there are now many ways of gaining qualifications at college, on a full- or part-time basis.

It is possible, for example, to take NVQs/SVQs Levels 1, 2 and 3 for chef training in food preparation, on a one-year full-time or two-year part-time course at some colleges. You can specialise in areas such as kitchen, larder, confectionery and patisserie.

As a young person leaving school, you might train as a chef via an apprenticeship (Skillseeker in Scotland). However, it is possible to train as a chef at any age. Experience in preparing food, or in customer service, may be an advantage.

Making the Grade: In larger organisations, NVQs/SVQs or plenty of experience in the job, can help you work your way up to head chef. In smaller businesses, though, there may not be any promotion prospects and progression means moving to another employer.

Some chefs eventually open their own restaurants or bars. They can also lecture or teach, train in nutrition or food technology, or work as advisers for food manufacturers.

Personal Qualities: To succeed as a chef, you would need to enjoy cooking, stay calm while working under pressure and use your creativity and imagination to devise menus and present your cooking in an attractive way.

You should have a passion for food but you must also relate this to running your kitchen as a profitable business.

Looking Ahead: There are around 30,000 vacancies for chefs in Britain and this number is thought to be rising. There are many opportunities to train and work in hotels, restaurants and bars. About a third of the restaurants are found in the south east of England, but there is no shortage of opportunities in most towns and cities.

More than half of the UK's restaurants are owner-managed or run in partnership and many are owned and run by chefs.

Alternative Suggestions: You might also consider training as a baker, catering/restaurant manager, food scientist/ technologist or hotel manager.

Take-home Pay: A commis chef will probably earn between £9,000 and £16,000, while a sous chef could earn between

£14,000 and £26,000. Head chefs (chefs de cuisine) can earn anything from around £25,000 to £50,000 plus.

Effects: The basic working week is 40 hours, but there may also be overtime during busy periods. A chef's job usually involves working shifts or split shifts, where staff work in the morning and then come in again for the evening. Most chefs have to work late into the evening and during weekends and bank holidays.

Large, busy kitchens are hot, steamy, noisy and hectic places to work and chefs can be under a lot of pressure to prepare meals quickly without sacrificing quality. They are on their feet in the kitchen for most of the time.

Leisure Services Manager

Leisure services managers may be responsible for one or more facilities such as swimming and leisure pools, sports halls, outdoor sports areas, gymnasia, ski slopes, ice rinks, 10-pin bowling alleys, restaurants and bars. The work could include running a leisure centre on a day-to-day basis, recruiting and supervising staff, organising, advertising and promoting events and managing budgets and controlling finances.

Entry Level: Most leisure services managers have professional qualifications or degrees and at least five years' relevant experience. Graduates and non-graduates often enter the work at lower, middle, assistant or trainee manager level and work towards professional qualifications while in employment.

For a degree course in a leisure management subject, you would normally need at least two A levels/three H grades and three GCSEs/two S grades (A-C/1-3) in other subjects, usually including English and maths, or equivalent qualifications. Experience of leisure services work is important before applying for any full-time post. This may be gained either part-time or by doing voluntary work, for example on summer holiday schemes for children, or as a part-time instructor of fitness or sports classes.

Making the Grade: A graduate training position with one of the larger employers would give you the chance to get the necessary experience to become a manager while studying for professional qualifications offered by the Institute of Leisure and Amenity Management or the Institute of Sport and Recreation Management. Similarly, even without a degree, you can train on the job and study for relevant qualifications, working your way up to trainee or assistant manager and eventually leisure services manager.

Personal Qualities: As a leisure services manager, you should have an interest in promoting sport and fitness, although active sporting ability is not essential. You must have organisational and planning abilities, good interpersonal skills for dealing with staff and customers and the ability to prepare accounts and manage budgets.

You must also be skilled at marketing your facilities and promoting special events.

Looking Ahead: Leisure is a growing industry. There are now some 5,000 leisure centres in the UK with about 11,500 managers. The largest centres may employ up to 100 staff altogether, with a number of managers. About 70% employ fewer than 10 people and one manager might be responsible for all facilities and activities. There is often strong competition for management jobs.

There are employment opportunities in privately-owned leisure centres, those owned by local authorities (many of which are privately run) and workplace clubs, including those run by very large companies or organisations. Similar management opportunities exist in theme parks and outdoor activity centres.

Alternative Suggestions: Other possibilities might include marketing executive, PE teacher, public relations officer or sports coach. The Hospitality and Catering or Leisure and Tourism industries present Global Opportunites.

Take-home Pay: Salaries very widely, according to the size and location of the leisure services provision you are managing. An assistant manager usually starts on around £14,000 to £19,000 a year. This could rise to £20,000 to £25,000 for a newly-appointed manager and to £40,000 plus for an experienced manager in a senior position.

Effects: Your working hours would almost certainly be irregular and could include early mornings, evenings, weekends and bank holidays. You would also have to be on call for special events and emergencies.

Baggage Porters and Bellhops

Overview: Baggage porters and bellhops handle luggage for travellers at transportation terminals or for guests at hotels.

After a long flight or road trip, the last thing you want to do is lug your heavy bags up to your room. Even if you can find a handtruck, it's not so easy to steer one of those things when your eyes are bleary from travel. Sometimes it's just best to leave it up to the professionals.

Bellhops escort newly-arrived guests to hotel rooms. They assist guests with small luggage. They explain specific features about the room, such as how to operate the television. Bellhops provide information about hotel facilities and local points of interest. They deliver messages and room service as well as pick up laundry for cleaning. Bellhops call taxicabs and courtesy vans for guests and may park their cars. They may also supply guests with travel information, such as bus routes, schedules and rates. In addition, bellhops maintain the security of the hotel. They may visit the rooms of guests who are making too much noise. They watch for thieves and may discourage people who are not guests from loitering around the hotel.

Baggage porters deliver luggage to and from hotel rooms using a hand truck. Porters often set up rooms for conferences and meetings. Porters escort guests to their rooms when the bellhop is busy. Porters also are in charge of luggage storage rooms. Guests sometimes store their luggage after they check out of their rooms. Porters fill out baggage claim checks and give them to guests. In addition, porters assist guests in packaging and shipping parcels.

Porters may also help travellers at airports, train stations and bus depots. They check luggage in. They may also help direct travellers to luggage claims and security check points.

Work Activities: The following list of occupational tasks is specific to this career.

- Move luggage to and from rooms, loading areas, or transportation terminals.
- Supply guests or travellers with directions, travel information and other information.
- Greet and escort arriving hotel guests to their rooms.
- Help physically challenged travellers and guests with special needs.
- Inspect guests' rooms and explain features, such as night-lock and operation of television.
- Complete and attach baggage claim checks and complete baggage insurance forms.
- Pick up guests' clothing to be laundered or repaired.
- Deliver messages and room service orders.
- Call cabs or shuttles for guests.
- Set up display tables, racks, or shelves for conferences.
- Work with security teams at transportation terminals and hotels.

People in this career perform the following list of tasks, but the tasks are common to many occupations.

- Identify objects, actions and events.
- Work with the public.
- Judge the value of objects, services, or people.
- Perform activities that use the whole body.
- Handle and move objects.
- Communicate with supervisors, peers, or subordinates.
- Monitor events, materials and surroundings.
- Make decisions and solve problems.
- Get information needed to do the job.
- Analyze data or information
- Update and use job-related knowledge.
- Establish and maintain relationships.
- Process information.
- Explain the meaning of information to others.
- Resolve conflicts and negotiate with others.
- Communicate with people from outside the organization.

Working Conditions: In a typical work setting, people in this career:

Interpersonal Relationships:

- Have a high level of social interaction. They constantly interact with guests and other hotel staff.
- Encounter angry or discourteous travellers every week.
- Communicate with hotel guests everyday by telephone.
- Always work as part of a team that provides service to guests.

Physical Work Conditions:

- Always wear uniforms.
- Mostly work outdoors, under a cover.
- Are exposed to hot and cold temperatures depending on the season.
- Work in cramped places on a weekly basis while loading and stowing luggage.
- Are always exposed to extremely bright or inadequate lighting, especially when working at night.
- Are exposed to automobile exhaust and other environmental pollution everyday.

Work Performance:

- Must finish all details of the job so that guests are satisfied.
- Must be accurate in their work so that guests receive the right luggage.
- Can set some tasks and goals without consulting a supervisor.
- Meet strict deadlines everyday to make sure people and baggage make their travel connections.
- Rarely consult a supervisor before making a decision.

Hours/Travel:

- May work part time or full time.
- May work days, evenings, weekends and holidays.

Physical Demand: People in this career frequently:

- Walk or run.

- Stand for long periods of time.
- Repeat the same movements.
- Bend or twist their body.

It is important for people in this career to be able to:

- Understand the speech of another person.
- Speak clearly so listeners can understand.
- Use muscles to lift, push, pull, or carry heavy objects.
- Use stomach and lower back muscles to support the body for long periods without getting tired.
- Coordinate movement of several parts of the body, such as arms and legs, while the body is moving.
- Be physically active for long periods without getting tired or out of breath.
- Bend, stretch, twist, or reach out.
- Move two or more limbs together (for example, two arms, two legs, or one leg and one arm) while remaining in place.

It is not as important, but still necessary, for people in this career to be able to:

- See details of objects that are nearby or a few feet away.
- Use one or two hands to grasp, move, or assemble objects.
- Move arms and legs quickly.
- Use muscles for extended periods without getting tired.
- Hold the arm and hand in one position or hold the hand steady while moving the arm.
- Focus on one source of sound and ignore others.

Skills and Abilities: People in this career need to:

Communicate

- Express ideas clearly when speaking or writing.
- Listen to others, understand and ask questions.
- Read and understand work-related materials.

Reason and Problem Solve:

- Notice when something is wrong or is likely to go wrong.
- Analyze ideas and use logic to determine their strengths and weaknesses.

- Understand new information or materials by studying and working with them.
- Concentrate and not be distracted while performing a task.
- Use reasoning to discover answers to problems.
- Follow guidelines to arrange objects or actions in a certain order.
- Judge the costs and benefits of a possible action.
- Identify problems and review information. Develop, review and apply solutions.

Manage Oneself, People, Time and Things:

- Check how well one is learning or doing something.
- Manage the time of self and others.

Work with People:

- Look for ways to help people.
- Be aware of others¿ reactions and change behaviour in relation to them.
- Use several methods to learn or teach new things.

Knowledge: People in this career need knowledge in the following areas:

- Customer and Personal Service: Knowledge of providing special services to customers based on their needs.
- English Language: Knowledge of the meaning, spelling and use of the English language.
- Transportation: Knowledge of ways to move people, goods, or materials. This may be by air, rail, sea, or road.
- Telecommunications: Knowledge of the equipment that is used to send messages as electronic impulses. Examples include radio, television, telegraph and cable.
- Public Safety and Security: Knowledge of protecting people, data and property.

Interests: People in this career are people who tend to:

- Consider relationships important. They like to work in a friendly, non-competitive environment. They like to do things for other people. They prefer jobs where they are

not pressured to do things that go against their sense of right and wrong.

- Consider support from their employer important. They like to be treated fairly and have supervisors who will back them up. They prefer jobs where they are trained well.
- Have enterprising interests. They like work activities that involve starting up and carrying out projects, especially in business. They like to lead and persuade others, make decisions and take risks for profit.
- Have realistic interests. They like work activities that include practical, hands-on problems and solutions. They like to work with plants, animals and physical materials such as wood, tools and machinery. They often prefer to work outside.
- Have social interests. They like work activities that assist others and promote learning and personal development. They like to communicate with others: to teach, give advice, help, or otherwise be of service to others.

Preparation: To work as a baggage porter or bellhop, you must:

have a high school diploma or GED;

complete on-the-job training; and

have good interpersonal skills.

Formal Education: No formal education is required beyond high school. Knowledge of a language other than English can be helpful in hotels that have guests from other countries.

On-the-job Training: Baggage porters and bellhops usually receive informal, on-the-job training from an experienced worker. On the job, you learn:

how to greet hotel guests;

customer service;

hotel services; and

hotel policies.

Bakers

Overview: Bakers mix and bake ingredients to produce breads, pastries and other baked goods.

The average wedding cake is usually a simple, three-tiered affair. On average, it probably weighs around 25 pounds. What would you do if your cake weighed seven and a half tons? Somebody's cake actually did weigh that much. In early 2004, a shopping and convention company set out to bake the world's largest cake. Its five tiers reached 17 feet high - that's taller than most rooms! Whoever baked this cake surely put in a lot of overtime.

Some bakers work in kitchens in restaurants, grocery stores and bakery shops. Other bakers work for companies that manufacture large quantities of baked goods. These packaged goods are then sold through businesses such as grocery stores. Both types of bakers perform similar tasks but on a different scale. For example, bakers who work for manufacturing companies use large ovens and mixing devices. They follow recipes that produce large numbers of the same item.

Bakers check their production schedule to determine the variety and quantity of goods to bake that day. Next, they measure flour and other ingredients into various-sized containers, following recipes. Bakers sometimes mix ingredients by hand, but usually use electric mixers or mixing machines. Then they roll, shape and cut the dough. Bakers use rolling pins to roll pie crust thin, then cut it to fit pie pans. They use cookie cutters to cut cookies. They use their hands to mold and shape bread dough. When baking pies, bakers cut and peel fruit fillings. Then they mix or sometimes cook the fillings and pour them into pie shells.

Bakers select the appropriate pans for various baked goods. They place the dough in pans, molds, or on sheets and bake it in the oven. They set the controls and adjust the drafts. They may also observe products as they bake, checking colour and adjusting controls. When groups of items are done, bakers mix icings and select toppings. Then they decorate cakes, pastries, or breads using spatulas or brushes. Sometimes they sprinkle sugar or seeded toppings on cookies or breads.

Some bakers develop new recipes of their own. This is more likely for bakers who work for manufacturing companies.

Work Activities: The following list of occupational tasks is specific to this career.

- Check production schedule to determine variety and quantity of goods to bake.
- Measure and mix ingredients to form dough or batter. Follow recipes.
- Roll, cut and shape dough to form rolls, pie crusts, tarts, cookies and other products.
- Cut, peel and prepare fruit for pie fillings.
- Place dough in pans, molds, or on sheets and bake in oven. Observe products while cooking and adjust ovens.
- Mix icings and other toppings and decorate cakes, pastries and other baked goods.
- Use a variety of kitchen tools, including electric mixers, pans, rolling pins and cutting tools.
- May develop new recipes.

People in this career perform the following list of tasks, but the tasks are common to many occupations.

- Monitor events, materials and surroundings.
- Handle and move objects.
- Get information needed to do the job.
- Control machines and processes.
- Carry out ideas, programmes, systems, or products.
- Perform activities that use the whole body.

Working Conditions: In a typical work setting, people in this career:

Interpersonal Relationships:

- Have a low level of social contact. They work mostly with baking tools and ingredients.

Physical Work Conditions:

- Always work indoors.
- Are sometimes exposed to hazardous situations, depending on the work setting. Bakers who produce large quantities

for manufacturing companies are more likely to be exposed to cuts and minor burns. However, injuries are usually slight.

- Sometimes wear a special uniform.

Work Performance:

- Must be sure that all details are done and their work is exact. Leaving out an ingredient could ruin products.
- Repeat the same physical activities, such as kneading and rolling dough.
- Must allow the speed of equipment to determine the work pace. For example, bakers must plan work so that new batches can be prepared while others bake.

Hours/Travel:

- May work part time or full time.
- May work early mornings, late evenings, holidays and weekends. This is more likely for bakers who work in restaurants, grocery stores and bakery shops.

Physical Demands: People in this career frequently:

- Stand for long periods of time.
- Use hands to handle, control, or feel objects, tools, or controls.
- Repeat the same movements over and over.

It is important for people in this career to be able to:

- Use fingers or hands to grasp, move, or assemble small objects.
- Make fast, repeated movements of fingers, hands and wrists.

It is not as important, but still necessary, for people in this career to be able to:

- See differences between colours, shades and brightness.
- See details of objects that are less than a few feet away.
- Hear sounds and recognize the difference between them.
- Hold the arm and hand in one position or hold the hand steady while moving the arm.

- Make quick, precise adjustments to machine controls.
- Bend, stretch, twist, or reach out.
- Move two or more limbs together (for example, two arms, two legs, or one leg and one arm) while remaining in place.
- React quickly using hands, fingers, or feet.
- Use muscles to lift, push, pull, or carry heavy objects.
- Use stomach and lower back muscles to support the body for long periods without getting tired.

Skills and Abilities: People in this career need to:

Communicate

- Read and understand work-related materials.

Reason and Problem Solve:

- Follow guidelines to arrange objects or actions in a certain order.

Use Math and Science:

- Use math skills to solve problems.

Work with Things:

- Operate and control equipment.
- Inspect and evaluate the quality of products.

Knowledge: People in this career need knowledge in the following areas:

- Production and Processing: Knowledge of how products are made and supplied.
- Food Production: Knowledge of planting, growing and harvesting food for eating.

Interests: People in this career are people who tend to:

- Consider support from their employer important. They like to be treated fairly and have supervisors who will back them up. They prefer jobs where they are trained well.
- Consider relationships important. They like to work in a friendly, non-competitive environment. They like to do things for other people. They prefer jobs where they are

not pressured to do things that go against their sense of right and wrong.

- Have realistic interests. They like work activities that include practical, hands-on problems and solutions. They like to work with plants, animals and physical materials such as wood, tools and machinery. They often prefer to work outside.
- Have enterprising interests. They like work activities that involve starting up and carrying out projects, especially in business. They like to lead and persuade others, make decisions and take risks for profit.
- Have artistic interests. They like work activities that deal with artistic forms, designs and patterns. They prefer work which allows for self expression.

Preparation

To work as a baker, you must:

have a high school diploma or GED;

complete formal training;

complete on-the-job training; and

have a good sense of smell and taste.

Formal Education: No formal education is required beyond high school for bakers. However, some bakers enrol in formal training programmes. Professional technical schools, two-year colleges and special culinary schools offer courses.

Culinary training includes courses in menu planning, food preparation and the selection and storage of food. Some programmes teach you how to bake specialty items such as pastries and gourmet breads. Training includes hands-on experience. Many programmes include courses in business management.

On-the-job Training: Most bakers learn their skills on the job from an experienced worker. You begin as a baker trainee. Training includes:

selecting and preparing ingredients;

baking;

decorating cakes;

baking processes; and

handling food.

Training lasts from one week to two months. Some employers train apprentices. After training, an experienced baker supervises your work. As you gain experience you receive more difficult tasks and more independence.

Military Training: The military is a good source of training for this occupation. In the military, you learn how to order food supplies, prepare baked items and handle food properly.

Helpful High School Courses: A high school degree is almost always required to work in this occupation. You should take courses in high school that prepare you to earn a high school diploma. This includes courses in English, math, science and social studies. You also need to take courses in physical education, health and applied art or second language.

Below is a list of high school courses that will help prepare you for this specific occupation. While you do not have to take all of them, you should consider them in planning for high school. Some of these courses are also available at colleges and technical schools.

Bartenders

Overview: Bartenders prepare and serve drinks to customers in bars and restaurants.

Did you know there are more than 1,000 drink recipes? The number of martini recipes alone is astounding. Add to this the number of microbrewed beers and wines and you've got a cornucopia of drinks on your hands. Those who have been pouring drinks for years are practically encyclopedias of wine, beer and spirits.

Bartenders prepare standard mixed drinks and pour wine and beer. They also prepare mixed drinks to match customers¿ specific orders. Most bartenders know dozens of drink recipes. They must be able to prepare drinks quickly, accurately and without waste. Some large restaurants use machines that create drinks. Bartenders who use these machines just push a button.

However, they must know how to prepare drinks in case the machine breaks. In most bars and many restaurants, bartenders take orders directly from customers. However, in some places they receive drink orders from waiters and waitresses.

In addition to serving drinks, bartenders collect payments and operate cash registers. They also clean up after customers and clean their work area. They often serve food to customers seated at the bar. Bartenders check identification of customers. Bartenders must be sure customers meet age requirements for the purchase of alcohol and tobacco products. They also make sure customers do not drink too much alcohol.

Bartenders are in charge of ordering and maintaining liquor and bar supplies. They often form attractive displays out of bottles and glassware. Bartenders wash the glassware and utensils after each use.

Other titles and keywords for this career.

Work Activities: The following list of occupational tasks is specific to this career.

- Collect payment and operate a cash register.
- Check identification of customers to make sure they meet age requirements for purchase of alcohol.
- Determine when a customer has had too much alcohol and try to stop them from drinking more.
- Wash glassware and utensils after each use. Clean bars, tables and work areas.
- Take drink orders from customers and serving staff.
- Pour wine and beer.
- Mix ingredients to prepare drinks and prepare garnishes.
- Order and maintain liquor and bar supplies.
- Manage bar operations and supervise staff.
- Plan displays and bar menus.
- Prepare appetizers, such as nuts, pickles, or cheese.
- Serve food to customers seated at the bar.
- Create drink recipes.

People in this career perform the following list of tasks, but the tasks are common to many occupations.

- Work with the public.
- Communicate with people from outside the organization.
- Establish and maintain relationships.
- Identify objects, actions and events.
- Communicate with supervisors, peers, or subordinates.
- Get information needed to do the job.
- Judge the value of objects, services, or people.
- Convince others to buy goods or change their minds or actions.
- Perform activities that use the whole body.
- Monitor events, materials and surroundings.
- Resolve conflicts and negotiate with others.
- Make decisions and solve problems.
- Update and use job-related knowledge.
- Handle and move objects.
- Inspect equipment, structures and materials.
- Assist and care for others.
- Estimate sizes, quantities, time, cost, or materials needed.

Working Conditions: In a typical work setting, people in this career:

Interpersonal Relationships:

- Have a high level of social contact. They constantly work with customers and food service staff.
- Are sometimes placed in conflict situations.
- Deal with unpleasant, angry, or discourteous people on a weekly basis.
- Are responsible for the health and safety of customers and staff. They make sure people do not drink too much alcohol. They also make sure that glassware is cleaned properly.
- Have daily face-to-face discussions with customers and staff.
- Communicate weekly using the telephone to make supply orders.

Physical Work Conditions:

- Mostly work indoors. They may occasionally work outdoors if tending bar at a party.
- Are sometimes exposed to sounds and noise levels that are distracting and uncomfortable.
- Sometimes wear a uniform.
- Work very near other people. They have very little space between self and others.

Work Performance:

- Must be exact in their work. They must be able to mix drinks accurately, quickly and without waste.
- Rarely consult a supervisor before making a decision or setting tasks.

Hours/Travel:

- Work less than 40 hours per week.
- May work days, nights, weekends and holidays.
- May be required to work split shifts. For example, they might work from 11 a.m. to 2 p.m. and 5 p.m. to 10 p.m., with time off in between.

Physical Demands: People in this career frequently:

- Stand and walk for long periods of time.
- Use hands to handle, control, or feel objects, tools, or controls.
- Repeat the same movements over and over.

It is important for people in this career to be able to:

- Understand the speech of another person.
- See details of objects that are less than a few feet away.
- Speak clearly so listeners can understand.
- Use stomach and lower back muscles to support the body for long periods without getting tired.
- Use hands and fingers to grasp, move, or assemble objects.
- Hold the arm and hand in one position or hold the hand steady while moving the arm.

It is not as important, but still necessary, for people in this career to be able to:

- Be physically active for long periods without getting tired or out of breath.
- Use muscles to lift, push, pull, or carry heavy objects.
- Coordinate movement of several parts of the body, such as arms and legs, while the body is moving or remaining in one place.
- Move two or more limbs together (for example, two arms, two legs, or one leg and one arm) while remaining in place.
- Bend, stretch, twist, or reach out.
- Use fingers to grasp, move, or assemble very small objects.
- Focus on one source of sound and ignore others.
- Move arms and legs quickly.
- Determine the distance between objects.
- See details of objects that are more than a few feet away.
- See differences between colours, shades and brightness.
- Make quick, precise adjustments to machine controls.

Skills and Abilities: People in this career need to:

Communicate

- Understand spoken information and ask questions as needed.
- Express ideas clearly when speaking.
- Read and understand work-related materials.

Reason and Problem Solve:

- Notice when something is wrong or is likely to go wrong.
- Follow guidelines to arrange objects or actions in a certain order.
- Analyze ideas and use logic to determine their strengths and weaknesses.
- Remember information such as words, numbers, pictures and procedures.
- Judge the costs and benefits of a possible action.

- Think of new ideas or original and creative ways to solve problems.
- Understand new information or materials by studying and working with them.
- Use reasoning to discover answers to problems.

Use Math and Science:

- Use math skills to solve problems.

Manage Oneself, People, Time and Things:

- Check how well one is doing something.

Work with People:

- Be aware of others¿ reactions and change behaviour in relation to them.
- Look for ways to help people.
- Use several methods to learn or teach new things.
- Persuade others to approach things differently.
- Solve problems by bringing others together to discuss differences.

Knowledge: People in this career need knowledge in the following areas:

- Customer and Personal Service: Knowledge of providing special services to customers based on their needs.
- Psychology: Knowledge of people, their actions and mental processes. This may include knowledge of how to treat emotional and behavioural problems.
- Mathematics: Knowledge of the rules and uses of numbers. Areas of knowledge include arithmetic, algebra, geometry and statistics.
- Sales and Marketing: Knowledge of advertising and selling products and services.

Interests: People in this career are people who tend to:

- Consider relationships important. They like to work in a friendly, non-competitive environment. They like to do things for other people. They prefer jobs where they are not pressured to do things that go against their sense of right and wrong.

- Consider support from their employer important. They like to be treated fairly and have supervisors who will back them up. They prefer jobs where they are trained well.
- Have enterprising interests. They like work activities that involve starting up and carrying out projects, especially in business. They like to lead and persuade others, make decisions and take risks for profit.
- Have social interests. They like work activities that assist others and promote learning and personal development. They like to communicate with others: to teach, give advice, help, or otherwise be of service to others.
- Have realistic interests. They like work activities that include practical, hands-on problems and solutions. They like to work with plants, animals and physical materials such as wood, tools and machinery. They often prefer to work outside.

Preparation: To work as a bartender, you need:

a high school diploma or GED;

to be at least 21 years old;

on-the-job training;

excellent interpersonal and communication skills; and

little or no previous work experience.

Formal Education: There are no formal education requirements beyond high school. However, you can get a bartending certificate from a professional technical school. Courses include information about state and local laws, mixing drinks and stocking a bar.

On-the-job Training: Most bartenders learn their skills on the job from an experienced worker. Training includes:

mixing drinks;

providing customer service;

using equipment needed for the job; and

handling food properly.

Training lasts from one week to two months. After training, an experienced worker supervises your work. As you gain experience, you receive less supervision.

Helpful High School Courses: Although a high school degree is usually not required to work in this occupation, it is important that you receive one to keep your career options open. Courses in English, math, science and social studies will prepare you to graduate from high school. You also need to take courses in physical education, health and applied art or a second language.

Below is a list of high school courses that will help prepare you for this specific occupation. While you do not have to take all of them, you should consider them in planning for high school. Some of these courses are also available at colleges and technical schools.

Business

Recordkeeping

Accounting

Computer and Information Sciences

Basic Computer

General Computer Applications

Business Computer Applications

Health and Safety Education

Health Education

Community Health

Safety and First Aid

Life and Physical Sciences

Chemistry

Mathematics

General Math

Business Math

Occupational Family and Consumer Sciences

Food Service

Food Service and Nutrition

Occupational Family and Consumer Sciences Work Experience

Social Sciences and History

Business Law

Hiring Practices

Employers prefer to hire people who are 25 or older. They prefer bartenders who have a neat, clean appearance and a courteous, outgoing manner. Many employers prefer bartenders to have a high school diploma or GED. They may also prefer those who have taken bartending courses.

Bartenders must know state and local laws about the sale of alcoholic beverages. Some states require bartenders to be certified in alcohol awareness. In states where certification is not required, employers may prefer applicants who have this knowledge. Most bartending courses include this certification in their training programmes.

Licensing / Certification: No State of Minnesota license requirements are found for this career.

Wages: Pay varies with the bartender's duties, the type of establishment and the type of clients. Bartenders employed in public bars may receive more than half of their earnings from tips. Bartenders who do not interact directly with the customers are often paid higher hourly wages. This is because they rarely receive tips. Full-time bartenders may receive paid vacation, sick leave and health insurance. Part-time workers generally do not receive benefits. Employers may provide meals and uniforms.

For more current and specific wage data, refer to the following Regional Wage Comparison Chart(s) produced by the Occupational Employment Statistics (OES) survey:

Bartenders

Employment: In Minnesota, about 15,910 bartenders work in this large occupation.

Nationally, about 474,400 bartenders work in this medium-sized occupation.

Jobs for bartenders are located throughout the country. However, most jobs are found in large cities and tourist areas. Vacation resorts offer seasonal employment.

Major employers:

Restaurants

Bars

Hotels

Country clubs

Counter Attendants

Overview: Counter attendants work at counters in coffee shops and small restaurants. They also work in cafeterias.

There is a famous episode of the hit TV show "Seinfeld" where each character becomes obsessed with a certain restaurant's soup. It seems the whole city lined up to get a bowl of the bisque to go. Yet, the counter attendant and chef had very strict rules about talking and ordering. If you didn't follow them precisely, you heard the dreaded words: "No soup for you!" Thankfully, in real life it's a little less stressful to order your favourite soup, sandwich, or iced coffee drink.

Counter attendants greet customers and write down meal orders on tickets. If coffee or other beverages are ordered, counter attendants pour and serve them. They take or call food orders to the kitchen. They may prepare sandwiches, salads and other items from the menu. If necessary, they add garnishes, such as fruit, to the plate. After the food is prepared, counter attendants serve it to customers. In some restaurants, they call out customers' names so they know to pick up their orders. Sometimes counter attendants wrap food so customers can take it with them.

Counter attendants take food out of storage and place it in serving displays. Sometimes they cook or reheat food. Counter attendants refill beverages such as water, coffee, or soda. They brew coffee and prepare desserts for customers. When the meal is finished, counter attendants compute bills and give them to customers. They may also operate cash registers, receive payment and make change. At the end of the day, they balance the cash register and keep records of the day's receipts.

Counter attendants clean counter tops and food-serving areas. They sweep floors and clean equipment. When containers of salt, pepper and sugar are running low, attendants restock them. They order items such as napkins when supplies are low.

In cafeterias, counter attendants make sure food-serving containers are full. They notify kitchen workers when food is running low or if special orders are necessary. Sometimes they carve and serve meat. They ladle soup and serve other items to customers.

Other titles and keywords for this career.

Work Activities: The following list of occupational tasks is specific to this career.

- Compute bill, receive payment and provide change when necessary.
- Write down customer orders and take to cooks.
- Serve food to customers.
- Prepare and serve sandwiches, salads and some items on the menu.
- Wrap food for customers to take out.
- Clean serving areas and equipment.
- Prepare and serve drinks.
- Add relish or garnish to plates.
- Order supplies such as napkins to replenish stock.
- Select food items from storage areas and place them in serving areas.
- Carve meat.
- Notify kitchen workers of shortages or special orders.
- Restock food at serving stations.
- Keep records and balance cash register at end of shift.

People in this career perform the following list of tasks, but the tasks are common to many occupations.

- Work with the public.

- Identify objects, actions and events.
- Communicate with supervisors, peers, or subordinates.
- Get information needed to do the job.
- Convince others to buy goods or change their minds or actions.
- Establish and maintain relationships.
- Handle and move objects.
- Coordinate the work activities of others.
- Perform activities that use the whole body.
- Make decisions and solve problems.
- Process information.
- Resolve conflicts and negotiate with others.
- Teach others.
- Monitor events, materials and surroundings.
- Inspect equipment or materials.
- Control machines and processes.
- Evaluate information against standards.
- Communicate with people from outside the organization.
- Estimate sizes, quantities, time, cost, or materials needed.

Working Conditions: In a typical work setting, people in this career:

Interpersonal Relationships:

- Have a high level of social interaction with customers and coworkers.
- Are responsible for the health and safety of others. They must follow safe food handling rules.
- Are responsible for the work outcomes of others.
- Are sometimes placed in conflict situations where customers might become unpleasant or angry.
- Work as part of a team serves customers.
- Talk face-to-face with customers daily.
- Often use the telephone to take customer's orders.

Physical Work Conditions:

- Usually work indoors. Sometimes prepare and serve food outdoors.

- Sometimes wear a special uniform.
- Are sometimes exposed to hazardous situations when working in the kitchen. They may work near stoves, ovens and hot grease. They may use knives and slicing machines.
- Are sometimes exposed to sounds and noise levels that are distracting and uncomfortable.
- Work very near other people and have little space between self and others.

Work Performance:

- Must be exact in taking orders and packaging food. Mistakes result in unhappy customers.
- Must sometimes meet strict deadlines.
- Can make some decisions and set some tasks without talking to a supervisor.
- Make decisions that affect others on a weekly basis.
- Make decisions that strongly impact the image of their employer.

Hours/Travel:

- Often work part time, but may work full time.
- May work days, evenings, or weekends.

Physical Demands: People in this career frequently.

- Stand for long periods of time.
- Walk for long period of time when serving customers.
- Use their hands to handle, control, or feel objects, tools, or controls.
- Repeat the same movements.
- Bend or twist their body.

It is important for people in this career to be able to:

- Speak clearly so listeners can understand.
- Understand the speech of another person.
- See details of objects that are less than a few feet away.

It is not as important, but still necessary, for people in this career to be able to:

- Use one or two hands to grasp, move, or assemble objects.

- Be physically active for long periods without getting tired or out of breath.
- Use stomach and lower back muscles to support the body for long periods without getting tired.
- Hold the arm and hand in one position or hold the hand steady while moving the arm.
- Move two or more limbs together (for example, two arms, two legs, or one leg and one arm) while remaining in place.
- Bend, stretch, twist, or reach out.
- Use muscles to lift, push, pull, or carry heavy objects.
- Focus on one source of sound and ignore others.
- Move arms and legs quickly.
- See details of objects that are more than a few feet away.
- Make quick, precise adjustments to machine controls.
- Determine the distance between objects.
- Use muscles for extended periods without getting tired.

Skills and Abilities: People in this career need to:

Communicate

- Listen to others, understand and ask questions.
- Express ideas clearly when speaking and writing.
- Read and understand work-related materials.

Reason and Problem Solve:

- Follow guidelines to arrange objects or actions in a certain order.
- Notice when something is wrong or is likely to go wrong.
- Use reasoning to discover answers to problems.
- Concentrate and not be distracted while performing a task.

Use Math and Science:

- Use math skills to solve problems.

Manage Oneself, People, Time and Things:

- Manage the time of self and others.

Work with People:

- Use several methods to learn or teach new things.
- Be aware of others¿ reactions and change behaviour in relation to them.
- Look for ways to help people.

Knowledge: People in this career need knowledge in the following areas:

- Customer and Personal Service: Knowledge of providing special services to customers based on their needs.
- Food Production: Knowledge of planting, growing and harvesting food for eating.
- Mathematics: Knowledge of the rules and uses of numbers. Areas of knowledge include arithmetic, algebra, geometry and statistics.
- Sales and Marketing: Knowledge of advertising and selling products and services.
- English Language: Knowledge of the meaning, spelling and use of the English language.

Interests: People in this career are people who tend to:

- Consider relationships important. They like to work in a friendly, non-competitive environment. They like to do things for other people. They prefer jobs where they are not pressured to do things that go against their sense of right and wrong.
- Consider support from their employer important. They like to be treated fairly and have supervisors who will back them up. They prefer jobs where they are trained well.
- Have realistic interests. They like work activities that include practical, hands-on problems and solutions. They like to work with plants, animals and physical materials such as wood, tools and machinery. They often prefer to work outside.
- Have social interests. They like work activities that assist others and promote learning and personal development. They like to communicate with others: to teach, give advice, help, or otherwise be of service to others.

Preparation: To work as a counter attendant, you need:

on-the-job Training: Good communication skills; and little or no previous work experience.

On-the-job Training: Almost all counter attendants learn their skills on the job from an experienced worker. Training includes: taking and serving orders; using equipment necessary for the job; providing customer service; and studying restaurant policies. After training, another worker supervises your work. Training lasts from one week to two months.

Outlook: In Minnesota, the number of jobs for counter attendants is expected to grow faster than average through the year 2014.

Nationally, the number of jobs for counter attendants is expected to grow as fast as average through the year 2014.

The fastest growth will be in the fast food industry. More people are visiting these restaurants for lunch or dinner because they can get their food quickly. Full-service restaurants will also experience growth.

There will be many openings for counter attendants every year. Much of this is due to the fact that workers do not stay in this occupation for long.

	Employment	*Employment Change*		
	2002	2012	Number	Percent
National	2,614,300	3,062,300	448,000	17.1

Advancement Opportunities: Advancement opportunities for counter attendants are limited. Counter attendants may advance to work as assistant managers or restaurant managers.

Fast Food Cooks

Overview: Fast food cooks prepare food for customers at fast food restaurants.

Are you organized? Have quick reflexes? Think fast on your feet? Enjoy working with people? Then a job as a fast food cook might be for you.

Fast food cooks prepare a limited selection of food items, such as hamburgers, tacos and pizza. They know what to prepare next by reading a food order or listening to requests from coworkers. Cooks follow specific recipes when preparing items. Foods such as hamburgers and tacos require assembly. Fast food cooks add all the ingredients for these items. They often must follow a set order for adding the meat, sauce, cheese and other parts. Once they have made these items, fast food cooks either wrap them or put them on a plate or basket. Sometimes fast food cooks also place the wrapped food in bags for "to go" orders. Some fast food cooks serve the food to customers at a window or counter.

In some restaurants, fast food cooks do not do much actual cooking. Instead, they use precooked food. Cooks just remove the food from the bag, heat it and use it when assembling items. However, in other restaurants, fast food cooks slice food such as onions or meat. They also measure ingredients and prepare dishes. This may involve monitoring food in fryers, grills, or warming machines. Cooks adjust cooking temperatures so food does not burn. In addition to cooking, fast food cooks may prepare and serve drinks, such as coffee and sodas. They also clean their work area and equipment. They must maintain strict safety and sanitation standards. They also restock their workstations and make take deliveries of supplies.

Depending on the type of food establishment, they may directly take orders and receive payment.

Other titles and keywords for this career.

Work Activities: The following list of occupational tasks is specific to this career.

- Read food order slip or respond to verbal requests.
- Slice and measure food.
- Prepare food according to specific recipes.
- Monitor food in fryers and grills and regulate cooking temperatures.
- Cook, assemble, wrap and package food items.
- Serve food to customers at window or counter.
- Prepare and serve drinks, such as coffee and sodas.
- Clean work area and equipment. Maintain sanitation standards.

- Make sure all food prepared is of high quality and the right quantity.
- May take orders and receive payment from customers.
- Restock workstations and display cases.
- Take delivery of supplies.

People in this career perform the following list of tasks, but the tasks are common to many occupations.

- Get information needed to do the job.
- Judge the value of objects, services, or people.
- Perform activities that use the whole body.
- Monitor events, materials and surroundings.
- Communicate with supervisors, peers, or subordinates.
- Work with the public.
- Inspect equipment, structures, or materials.
- Handle and move objects.
- Organize, plan and prioritize work.
- Schedule work and activities.
- Make decisions and solve problems.
- Resolve conflicts and negotiate with others.

Working Conditions: In a typical work setting, people in this career:

Interpersonal Relationships:

- Have a medium level of social contact. They usually do not take orders directly from customers, but interact with wait staff, managers and other cooks.
- Are responsible for the health and safety of others.

Physical Work Conditions:

- Usually work indoors. May work outdoors at catered events or at an outdoor food stand, for example.
- Sometimes wear a special uniform.
- Are sometimes exposed to situations that cause cuts and burns or slips and falls. Injuries are usually slight, however.
- Work very near others, sometimes within a few feet or closer. Restaurant kitchens are often small spaces.

- May be exposed to distracting noises and sound levels from cooktops.

Work Performance:

- Must fully complete and be exact in their work. Improperly prepared food might make people sick.
- Must keep pace with the speed at which food is cooking.
- May repeat the same activities, especially making the same recipe over and over.
- Sometimes make decisions that affect co-workers and the company's reputation. They can make most decisions without talking to a supervisor first.
- Set most of their daily tasks and goals without talking to a supervisor first. Their tasks are often determined by food orders.
- Work in a competitive atmosphere. They may try to compete with each other over the speed at which is food is prepared.

Hours/Travel:

- May work early mornings, late evenings, holidays, weekends, or days.
- May work part time or full time. Most work about 40 hours.

Physical Demands:

People in this career frequently:

- Stand at fryers and grills for long periods of time.
- Walk or run in the kitchen to retrieve supplies for long periods of time.
- Repeat the same movements over and over.
- Use hands to handle, control, or feel objects, tools, or controls.
- Bend or twist their body.

It is important for people in this career to be able to:

- Understand the speech of another person.
- Use stomach and lower back muscles to support the body for long periods without getting tired.
- Use one or two hands to grasp, move, or assemble objects.

It is not as important, but still necessary, for people in this career to be able to::

- See details of objects that are less than a few feet away.
- Speak clearly so listeners can understand.
- Hold the arm and hand in one position or hold the hand steady while moving the arm.
- Be physically active for long periods without getting tired or out of breath.
- Make quick, precise adjustments to machine controls.
- Move two or more limbs together (for example, two arms, two legs, or one leg and one arm) while remaining in place.
- Use muscles to lift, push, pull, or carry heavy objects.
- Focus on one source of sound and ignore others.
- Coordinate movement of several parts of the body, such as arms and legs, while the body is moving.
- React quickly using hands, fingers, or feet.
- Bend, stretch, twist, or reach out.
- Move arms and legs quickly.
- Make fast, repeated movements of fingers, hands and wrists.
- Use fingers to grasp, move, or assemble very small objects.

Skills and Abilities: People in this career need to:

Communicate

- Listen to others, understand and ask questions.
- Read and understand written information.
- Express ideas clearly when speaking.

Reason and Problem Solve:

- Analyze ideas and use logic to determine their strengths and weaknesses.
- Follow guidelines to arrange objects or actions in a certain order.
- Judge the costs and benefits of a possible action.
- Notice when something is wrong or is likely to go wrong.

Use Math and Science:

- Use math skills to solve problems.

Manage Oneself, People, Time and Things:

- Check how well one is learning or doing something.

Work with People:

- Look for ways to help people.
- Use several methods to learn or teach others how to do something.
- Be aware of others¿ reactions and understand the possible causes.

Knowledge: People in this career need knowledge in the following areas:

- Customer and Personal Service: Knowledge of providing special services to customers based on their needs.
- Food Production: Knowledge of planting, growing and harvesting food for eating.
- Production and Processing: Knowledge of how products are made and supplied.
- Personnel and Human Resources: Knowledge of the department that is in charge of the relationship between a company and its employees. In particular, includes knowledge of the activities performed by the department.
- Sales and Marketing: Knowledge of advertising and selling products and services.

Interests: People in this career are people who tend to:

- Consider relationships important. They like to work in a friendly, non-competitive environment. They like to do things for other people. They prefer jobs where they are not pressured to do things that go against their sense of right and wrong.
- Consider support from their employer important. They like to be treated fairly and have supervisors who will back them up. They prefer jobs where they are trained well.
- Have realistic interests. They like work activities that include practical, hands-on problems and solutions. They

like to work with plants, animals and physical materials such as wood, tools and machinery. They often prefer to work outside.

- Have conventional interests. They like work activities that follow set procedures, routines and standards. They like to work with data and detail. They prefer working where there is a clear line of authority to follow.

Preparation: To work as a fast food cook, you need: on-the-job training; little or no previous work experience; and the ability to work as part of a team.

Work Experience: It is very helpful if you have experience working in a fast food restaurant.

On-the-job Training: Most fast food cooks learn their skills on the job from an experienced worker. Training includes: preparing menu items; and handling food safely.

After training, another worker supervises your work for a period. Training may last from one week to two months.

Outlook: In Minnesota, the number of jobs for fast food cooks is expected to grow faster than average through the year 2014.

Nationally, the number of jobs for fast food cooks is expected to grow as fast as average through the year 2014.

Americans will continue to eat out often, especially at fast food restaurants. Fast food cooks are assisted by workers who also wait on customers. This assistance limits the number of cooks each restaurant needs.

Despite the slow growth, jobs will be plentiful because of the need to replace workers who leave their jobs.

	Employment	*Employment Change*		
	2002	2012	Number	Percent
National	662,200	771,000	108,800	16.4

Advancement Opportunities: With experience, fast food cooks may advance to higher pay and seniority within a company. Some may move to supervisory positions. With more training and experience, fast food cooks can advance to a cook or chef position in a restaurant or other institution.

Food Preparation Workers

Overview: Food preparation workers get food ready for cooking or serving.

Ever make a veggie tray with dip? Sounds easy, right? Buy some carrots, celery, broccoli, cauliflower, radishes and a container of dip. Easy! Yes. Except now you have to clean all the veggies. Then you have to peel the carrots. Next, you have to cut them, along with the celery. Then you have to break apart the cauliflower and the broccoli. And then there's the radishes. How do people cut them so they look like flowers?

Food preparation workers make veggie trays and then some. Usually, though, the job goes much faster. They have bigger equipment, sharper knives and most importantly, experience.

Food preparation workers weigh, measure, clean, cut, or peel foods to prepare them for cooking. They work with all sorts of food, including vegetables, meat, fish and poultry. They often make salads and dressings. Food preparation workers also keep food cold or hot, depending on the circumstances. They usually prep food according to a supervisor's instructions. In some cases, menus change daily, so the food that needs to be prepared varies greatly. In addition, if workers are employed by a large cafeteria or restaurant, they may work in an assembly line.

Using customers' orders, food preparation workers prepare food and arrange it on serving dishes or in containers. They distribute food to waiters and waitresses to serve to customers. They also prepare and serve a variety of beverages, such as coffee, tea and soft drinks. Food preparation workers may also help cooks and chefs with tasks during busy times. They may also keep salad bars, buffet tables, salt and pepper shakers and utensil areas filled and stocked.

Food preparation workers clean and maintain work areas and equipment. They may also order, store and distribute food supplies, equipment and utensils. Some may keep records of how much food was used. They keep their work areas clean and often load and run large industrial dishwashers.

Other titles and keywords for this career.

Work Activities: The following list of occupational tasks is specific to this career.

- Clean, cut, or peel various foods to prepare for cooking or serving.
- Weigh or measure ingredients.
- Prepare foods according to customers' or supervisors' orders.
- Arrange food on serving dishes or in take-out containers.
- Give food to waiters and waitresses to serve to customers.
- Prepare and serve beverages.
- Help cooks and other kitchen staff with various tasks.
- Store food properly to prevent it from spoiling.
- Clean work areas and maintain equipment.
- Load and run dishwashing machines.
- Keep refrigerators, buffet tables and salad bars stocked.
- Organize and put away food supplies and equipment in their proper places.
- Keep records of how much food has been used.
- May order and distribute supplies.

People in this career perform the following list of tasks, but the tasks are common to many occupations.

- Communicate with supervisors, peers, or subordinates.
- Perform activities that use the whole body.
- Establish and maintain relationships.
- Work with the public.
- Get information needed to do the job.
- Identify objects, actions and events.
- Evaluate information against standards.
- Handle and move objects.
- Coordinate the work and activities of others.
- Estimate sizes, quantities, time, cost, or materials needed.
- Organize, plan and prioritize work.
- Assist and care for others.

- Judge the value of objects, services, or people.
- Monitor events, materials and surroundings.

Working Conditions: In a typical work setting, people in this career:

Interpersonal Relationships:

- Have a medium level of social contact. They work with customers and other staff, but also spend time alone preparing food.
- Communicate daily with supervisors and coworkers in person. Communicate less often by telephone, usually a few times per week.
- Are responsible for the health and safety of customers.
- Are somewhat responsible for the work of other workers.
- May occasionally deal with angry or discourteous customers.
- Almost always work in a group or as part of a team.

Physical Work Conditions:

- Nearly always work indoors.
- Wear protective gear, such as gloves and hair nets, on a weekly basis.
- Are sometimes exposed to hazardous situations that may result in cuts or minor burns.
- Are occasionally exposed to very hot or very cold temperatures. They work near large freezers and ovens.
- Work within a few feet of other workers. They usually share the same kitchen or prep room.

Work Performance:

- Must be very exact in their work to prevent safety hazards.
- Repeat the same motions.
- Make most decisions without consulting a supervisor. This is because tasks vary little from day to day.
- Can set some of their tasks and goals for the day, but usually receive instructions from a supervisor first. Menus often change, so workers must prep different food items.
- Abide by deadlines on a daily basis.

Hours/Travel:

- Usually work about 40 hours per week. Some work part time.
- Hours may include early mornings, late evenings, holidays and weekends.
- Generally work a set schedule.

Physical Demands: People in this career frequently:

- Stand or walk for long periods of time while preparing food.
- Use hands to handle, control, or feel objects, tools, or controls.
- Repeat the same movements over and over.
- Bend or twist their body.

It is important for people in this career to be able to:

- Hold the arm and hand in one position or hold the hand steady while moving the arm.
- Use one or two hands to grasp, move, or assemble objects.
- Understand the speech of another person.
- See details of objects that are less than a few feet away.
- Use muscles to lift, push, pull, or carry heavy objects.
- Use stomach and lower back muscles to support the body for long periods without getting tired.
- Speak clearly so listeners can understand.
- Bend, stretch, twist, or reach out.

It is not as important, but still necessary, for people in this career to be able to:

- Make fast, repeated movements of fingers, hands and wrists.
- See differences between colours, shades and brightness.
- Be physically active for long periods without getting tired or out of breath.
- Use fingers to grasp, move, or assemble very small objects.
- Make quick, precise adjustments to machine controls.
- Move two or more limbs together (for example, two arms,

two legs, or one leg and one arm) while remaining in place.

- Move arms and legs quickly.
- Focus on one source of sound and ignore others.
- Determine the distance between objects.
- Hear sounds and recognize the difference between them.
- Coordinate movement of several parts of the body, such as arms and legs, while the body is moving.
- See details of objects that are more than a few feet away.
- Use muscles for extended periods without getting tired.
- React quickly using hands, fingers, or feet.

Skills and Abilities: People in this career need to:

Communicate

- Listen to others, understand and ask questions.
- Read and understand work-related materials.
- Express ideas clearly when speaking.

Reason and Problem Solve:

- Follow guidelines to arrange objects or actions in a certain order.
- Use reasoning to discover answers to problems.
- Notice when something is wrong or is likely to go wrong.
- Combine several pieces of information and draw conclusions.

Use Math and Science:

- Use math skills to solve problems.

Work with People:

- Use several methods to teach others how to do something.
- Look for ways to help people.
- Be aware of others¿ reactions and change behaviour in relation to them.

Perceive and Visualize:

- Imagine how something will look if it is moved around or its parts are rearranged.
- Identify a pattern (a figure, object, word, or sound) that is hidden in distracting material.

Knowledge: People in this career need knowledge in the following areas:

- Customer and Personal Service: Knowledge of providing special services to customers based on their needs.
- Food Production: Knowledge of planting, growing and harvesting food for eating.
- Mathematics: Knowledge of the rules and uses of numbers. Areas of knowledge include arithmetic, algebra, geometry and statistics.
- English Language: Knowledge of the meaning, spelling and use of the English language.

Interests: People in this career are people who tend to:

- Consider relationships important. They like to work in a friendly, non-competitive environment. They like to do things for other people. They prefer jobs where they are not pressured to do things that go against their sense of right and wrong.
- Have realistic interests. They like work activities that include practical, hands-on problems and solutions. They like to work with plants, animals and physical materials such as wood, tools and machinery. They often prefer to work outside.
- Have conventional interests. They like work activities that follow set procedures, routines and standards. They like to work with data and detail. They prefer working where there is a clear line of authority to follow.

Preparation: To work as a food preparation worker, you need: on-the-job training; and little or no previous work experience.

On-the-job Training: Most food preparation workers learn their skills on the job from an experienced worker. Training includes:

how to prepare food;

cooking skills; and

food handling techniques.

After training, another worker closely supervises your work. Training may last from one week to two months.

Military Training: The military can be a good source of training for this occupation. Soldiers can be trained to prepare food to serve in military cafeterias.

Outlook: In Minnesota, the number of jobs for food preparation workers is expected to grow about as fast as average through the year 2014.

Nationally, the number of jobs for food preparation workers is expected to increase faster than average through the year 2014.

Demand will grow as people have more money to spend on dining out. Because there are more demands on their time, families are expected to go to fast food and informal restaurants more often. The number of affluent people over the age of 55 is also growing. These factors will increase the demand for restaurants and for workers who prepare food.

There will be plenty of job openings for food preparation workers. Job turnover is high due to low wages and the fact that most jobs are part-time.

	Employment	*Employment Change*		
	2002	2012	Number	Percent
National	888,500	1,063,700	175,200	19.7

Advancement Opportunities: Food preparation workers may advance to assistant cook or short-order cook positions. However, they must acquire some basic food preparation and cooking skills first.

Food Service Worker Supervisors

Overview: Food service worker supervisors direct and oversee the work of staff who prepare and serve food.

Did you know that each day, 7% of Americans go to McDonald's? Over 20% of Americans go to a fast-food restaurant for at least one meal on a daily basis. This creates the need for a lot of food service workers. And of course, someone needs to supervise these workers to make sure food is served hot and fast.

Food service supervisors manage workers who prepare and serve food and drinks. They also deal with customers and perform management tasks. Their duties vary based on where they work. Supervisors in large facilities often spend most of their time supervising other workers. They may also perform food preparation or service tasks, such as pouring wine or carving large roasts. Supervisors in smaller eating places often spend most of their time on management tasks.

Supervisors work closely with food service staff. They analyze work requirements and then assign workers to duties and workstations. They observe and evaluate workers and their work procedures. They try to ensure that customers receive quality standards and service. Food service supervisors also review staffing needs and decide when to hire new employees. They interview applicants and sometimes discharge those who are not doing their job. They also train staff in proper food preparation and service procedures.

Food service supervisors are often in charge of supplies and equipment. They take inventory and report shortages. They order supplies and make sure they are delivered on time. They may record data about purchases on forms or on computers. They often keep track of how much food has been sold on a daily basis. Supervisors also work with customers. In restaurants, they schedule parties or reservations and greet guests when they arrive. They often present bills and take payment from customers. Supervisors who work in hospitals make sure that patients who have special dietary needs get the right kinds of meals. Supervisors in all settings resolve customer complaints about food or service.

Food service supervisors often confer with managers or other staff. They plan details, such as menus and serving arrangements. They analyze the size of portions and how many workers they may need in the future. They discuss problems, such as theft or waste and set up methods for preventing these problems in the future. They also recommend changes in work procedures or worker performance. Their goal is to improve customer service and job safety.

Other titles and keywords for this career.

Work Activities: The following list of occupational tasks is specific to this career.

- Supervise and coordinate the activities of food preparation and service workers.
- Assign workers to duties and workstations based on work requirements.
- Observe and evaluate workers. Inspect equipment and work areas.
- Assess staffing needs and hire and discharge employees.
- Train workers in proper food preparation and service procedures.
- Take inventory of supplies and equipment and report shortages.
- Order equipment and supplies to ensure timely delivery.
- Schedule parties and reservations. Greet and escort guests.
- Present bills to customers and process payments.
- Resolve customer complaints about service.
- Gather and total cash receipts at the end of the day or shift.
- Confer with managers or other staff to plan future staff, equipment and supply needs.
- Recommend changes in work procedures or worker performance to improve service or job safety.
- Determine menus and portions and how to produce them. Estimate ingredients and supplies needed to make a recipe.
- Keep and update records of food and staff costs.
- Review operational problems, such as theft and waste. Set up methods for preventing these problems.
- May perform some food preparation and service tasks.

People in this career perform the following list of tasks, but the tasks are common to many occupations.

- Work with the public.
- Identify objects, actions and events.

- Get information needed to do the job.
- Make decisions and solve problems.
- Communicate with supervisors, peers, or subordinates.
- Establish and maintain relationships.
- Teach others.
- Evaluate information against standards.
- Resolve conflicts and negotiate with others.
- Convince others to buy goods or change their minds or actions.
- Monitor events, materials and surroundings.
- Guide, direct and motivate subordinates.
- Perform administrative tasks.
- Handle and move objects.
- Coordinate the work and activities of others.
- Perform activities that use the whole body.
- Inspect equipment, structures, or materials.
- Use computers.
- Communicate with people from outside the organization.
- Judge the value of objects, services, or people.

Working Conditions: In a typical work setting, people in this career:

Interpersonal Relationships:

- Have a high level of social contact. They work closely with the staff they supervise.
- Communicate with employees and customers by telephone and in person on a daily basis. They may occasionally communicate using letters and memos.
- Are placed in conflict situations on a weekly basis. They may deal with customers who are unpleasant, impolite, or angry.
- Regularly work in a group or as part of a team.
- Are substantially responsible for the work outcomes of those they supervise.
- Are greatly responsible for the health and safety of customers and other workers.

Physical Work Conditions:

- Nearly always work indoors, but may on rare occasions work outdoors.
- Are sometimes exposed to hazardous situations that may produce cuts or minor burns. This is because they often handle knives and work near hot surfaces, such as stoves and ovens.
- Are often exposed to distracting sounds and noisy conditions that may be uncomfortable. Restaurants and cafeterias are noisy, busy places.
- Are often exposed to very hot or very cold temperatures. They often work near large freezers and ovens.
- Wear protective or safety attire on a weekly basis. They may wear gloves, hair coverings and other similar equipment.
- Work very near others, perhaps within a foot of another person. They stand near other workers when preparing and handling food.

Work Performance:

- Must be sure that all details are done and their work is exact. Errors could result in a shortage of workers or supplies.
- Make decisions that strongly impact workers and the company's reputation. Restaurants often rely on reputation and word-of-mouth to attract and keep customers.
- Make decisions everyday that affect workers. They rarely consult superiors before doing so.
- Usually set most of their tasks and priorities for the day without consulting a superior. This is because many of the tasks are the same from day to day.
- Abide by weekly deadlines.
- Repeat the same activities over and over.

Hours/Travel:

- Generally, work a set schedule. They may work "split shifts." For example, they might work from 6 a.m. to 10 a.m. and 3 p.m. to 7 p.m., with time off in between.

- May work part time or full time. Most work full time, about 40 hours a week.
- May work evenings, weekends, or holidays.
- May work more conventional hours if employed in institutional food service facilities, such as schools.

Physical Demands:

People in this career frequently:

- Stand or walk for long periods of time.
- Repeat the same movements.
- Use hands to handle, control, or feel objects, tools, or controls.

It is important for people in this career to be able to:

- Speak clearly so listeners can understand.
- Understand the speech of another person.
- See details of objects that are less than a few feet away.

It is not as important, but still necessary, for people in this career to be able to:

- Use stomach and lower back muscles to support the body for long periods without getting tired.
- Hold the arm and hand in one position or hold the hand steady while moving the arm.
- Use one or two hands to grasp, move, or assemble objects.
- Be physically active for long periods without getting tired or out of breath.
- Coordinate movement of several parts of the body, such as arms and legs, while the body is moving.
- Bend, stretch, twist, or reach out.
- Move two or more limbs together (for example, two arms, two legs, or one leg and one arm) while remaining in place.
- See details of objects that are more than a few feet away.
- Focus on one source of sound and ignore others.
- Use muscles to lift, push, pull, or carry heavy objects.
- Move arms and legs quickly.
- Make quick, precise adjustments to machine controls.

Skills and Abilities: People in this career need to:

Communicate

- Express ideas clearly when speaking or writing.
- Listen to others, understand and ask questions.
- Read and understand written materials.

Reason and Problem Solve:

- Notice when something is wrong or is likely to go wrong.
- Develop rules or follow guidelines for arranging items.
- Use reasoning to discover answers to problems.
- Analyze ideas and use logic to determine their strengths and weaknesses.
- Understand new information or materials by studying and working with them.
- Combine several pieces of information and draw conclusions.
- Judge the costs and benefits of a possible action.

Use Math and Science:

- Use math skills to solve problems.

Manage Oneself, People, Time and Things:

- Manage the time of self and others.
- Check how well one is learning or doing something.
- Motivate, develop and direct people as they work.
- Go back and forth between two or more activities or sources of information without becoming confused.

Work with People:

- Use several methods to teach others how to do something.
- Look for ways to help people.
- Be aware of others¿ reactions and change behaviour in relation to them.

Work with Things:

- Maintain equipment on a routine basis. Determine when and what kind of maintenance is needed.
- Test and inspect products, services, or processes. Evaluate quality or performance.

- Watch gauges, dials and output to make sure a machine is working properly.

Knowledge: People in this career need knowledge in the following areas:

- Customer and Personal Service: Knowledge of providing special services to customers based on their needs.
- Administration and Management: Knowledge of managing the operations of a business, company, or group.
- Production and Processing: Knowledge of how products are made and supplied.
- Food Production: Knowledge of planting, growing and harvesting food for eating.
- Personnel and Human Resources: Knowledge of the department that is in charge of the relationship between a company and its employees. In particular, includes knowledge of the activities performed by the department.

Interests: People in this career are people who tend to:

- Consider independence important. They like to make decisions and try out ideas on their own. They prefer jobs where they can plan their work with little supervision.
- Consider relationships important. They like to work in a friendly, non-competitive environment. They like to do things for other people. They prefer jobs where they are not pressured to do things that go against their sense of right and wrong.
- Consider achievement important. They like to see the results of their work and to use their strongest abilities. They like to get a feeling of accomplishment from their work.
- Consider recognition important. They like to work in jobs which have opportunities for them to advance, be recognized for their work and direct and instruct others. They usually prefer jobs in which they are looked up to by others.
- Consider good working conditions important. They like jobs offering steady employment and good pay. They want employment that fits their individual work style.

They may prefer doing a variety of tasks, working alone, or being busy all the time.

- Have enterprising interests. They like work activities that involve starting up and carrying out projects, especially in business. They like to lead and persuade others, make decisions and take risks for profit.
- Have realistic interests. They like work activities that include practical, hands-on problems and solutions. They like to work with plants, animals and physical materials such as wood, tools and machinery. They often prefer to work outside.
- Have conventional interests. They like work activities that follow set procedures, routines and standards. They like to work with data and detail. They prefer working where there is a clear line of authority to follow.

Preparation: To work as a food service worker supervisor, you need: a high school diploma or GED; on-the-job training; good interpersonal and communication skills; and work experience in the food service industry.

Formal Education: For most food service worker supervisors there are no formal education requirements beyond high school. However, many supervisors have a bachelor's degree.

Many colleges and universities offer four-year programmes in restaurant and hotel management or food service management. In addition, many professional technical schools and two-year colleges offer food service management programmes. These programmes lead to a certificate or an associate degree. Both types of programmes offer courses in nutrition, food planning and food preparation. They also include courses in accounting, business management and computer science. Some programmes combine classroom study with experience in a restaurant setting.

Work Experience: Many food service worker supervisors have several years of experience working in restaurants.

On-the-job Training: Employers may offer short-term on-the-job training that lasts up to three months.

Supervisors may attend management training programmes. This is most likely for those who work for large restaurant chains.

Outlook: In Minnesota, the number of jobs for food service worker supervisors is expected to grow faster than average through the year 2014. Nationally, the number of jobs for food service worker supervisors is expected to grow as fast as average through the year 2014.

Job growth will be spurred by increases in the population, household income and leisure time. More income and leisure time allow people to take vacations and dine out more often. In addition, in an increasing number of families all parents work. These families are more likely to go out to eat. Thus, as more people eat out, the demand for supervisors should grow. In addition, growth in the elderly population will result in more food service supervisor jobs in nursing homes and residential care facilities.

	Employment	*Employment Change*		
	2002	2012	Number	Percent
National	772,600	901,200	128,600	16.6

Advancement Opportunities: Advancement for food service supervisors is limited in small establishments. However, they can advance by taking jobs with bigger companies or with institutional facilities, such as schools. Experienced supervisors in large restaurant chains may advance to manager jobs. Willingness to relocate is often important to advance to positions with more responsibility. Additional training or college education may be required for advancement.

Hotel Desk Clerks

Overview: Hotel desk clerks perform a variety of services for hotel guests.

Travelling can sometimes be a harrowing experience. Flights may be delayed or even cancelled. Driving over mountain passes can be a little frightening, or simply tiring after many hours on the road. Tickets, luggage and tempers alike might be lost. If you've ever have a trip like this, you know what a relief it is to finally get to the hotel. The clerk smiles, handles your check-in in a flash and hands you a key to heaven: your room. After a day of problems, you want to reach over and hug the clerk!

Hotel desk clerks work at the front desk in hotels, motels and resorts. They are responsible for making guests feel comfortable and welcome. They make advance reservations by telephone and greet guests when they arrive. They check guests in, assign their rooms and issue room keys. In small hotels, clerks give guests directions to their rooms and tell them where to park. In large hotels, they give instructions to bellhops who take guests to their rooms. In addition, clerks keep records of room assignments and availability. Records and reservations are usually kept on computers.

Hotel desk clerks assist guests in a variety of other ways. They answer questions about hotel services and policies. They answer questions about local restaurants, shopping, entertainment and travel. They may arrange taxis or tours for guests. When guests report problems with their rooms, clerks contact housekeeping or maintenance staff to take care of them. They often keep records of complaints and they may refer guests to managers if necessary. In addition, hotel desk clerks transfer incoming calls to guests¿ rooms and take messages when they are out. They may also sort mail for guests and make sure they receive it. In large hotels, clerks sometimes deposit guests¿ valuables in the hotel safe.

Hotel desk clerks are responsible for computing guests¿ bills. When a guest makes a reservation, they arrange how the guest will pay. Clerks post charges to guests¿ accounts for their rooms, phone calls and food. When guests check out, clerks prepare the bill, explain charges and collect payment. They almost always use computers for these tasks. Once again, they are responsible for creating a good impression for the hotel.

Hotel desk clerks who work in smaller hotels and motels may have additional duties. In some small hotels, clerks are responsible for all front office operations. For example, they may perform bookkeeping and laundry duties.

Other titles and keywords for this career.

Work Activities: The following list of occupational tasks is specific to this career.

- Take and confirm advance reservations by telephone. Establish how they will pay for the room.
- Greet and register guests and assign rooms.
- Issue room keys. Give room directions to guests or instructions to bellhop.
- Deposit guests' valuables in hotel safe, when available.
- Keep records of room assignments and availability.
- Answer questions about hotel services, policies and the community. May arrange tours or cabs.
- Contact housekeeping or maintenance staff when guests report problems or when rooms are ready to be cleaned.
- Transfer calls and receive messages, using telephone or switchboard.
- Date and sort incoming mail and messages. Make sure they reach guests.
- Use computers to take reservations, keep records and post charges to guests' accounts.
- Prepare bills, explain charges and collect payment at check-out.
- Keep records of guest comments or complaints. Refer guests to managers if necessary.
- May perform other duties, such as bookkeeping or laundry, in small hotels.

People in this career perform the following list of tasks, but the tasks are common to many occupations.

- Work with the public.
- Use computers.
- Communicate with supervisors, peers, or subordinates.
- Get information needed to do the job.
- Resolve conflicts and negotiate with others.
- Make decisions and solve problems.
- Document and record information.
- Communicate with people from outside the organization.

- Assist and care for others.
- Establish and maintain relationships.
- Perform administrative tasks.
- Process information.
- Judge the value of objects, services, or people.
- Organize, plan and prioritize work.
- Identify objects, actions and events.
- Explain the meaning of information to others.
- Analyze data or information.
- Update and use job-related knowledge.
- Evaluate information against standards.
- Convince others to buy goods or change their minds or actions.

Working Conditions: In a typical work setting, people in this career:

Interpersonal Relationships:

- Have a very high level of social contact. They interact frequently with guests in person and by telephone.
- Communicate by letters and memos on a weekly basis.
- Often deal with conflict situations in which they interact with unpleasant or angry people. Guests may dispute charges or policies.
- Are responsible for the results of their work.
- Regularly work in a group or as part of a team.

Physical Work Conditions:

- Often work indoors.
- Work near others, usually within a few feet.

Work Performance:

- Must be exact in their work so that guests are happy with the service.
- Make decisions that affect customers and other workers on a daily basis. They make most decisions without consulting a supervisor first.
- Can set some tasks without talking to a supervisor, but often consult a supervisor first.

- Repeat the same activities, such as operating a computer or talking on a telephone.

Hours/Travel:

- Usually work a set schedule.
- May work part time or full time. Most work full time.
- May work days, evenings, late night shifts, weekends and holidays.

Physical Demands:

People in this career frequently:

- Stand for long periods of time.
- Repeat the same movements.
- Use their hands to handle, control, or feel objects, tools, or controls.

It is important for people in this career to be able to:

- Speak clearly so listeners can understand.
- See details of objects that are less than a few feet away.
- Understand the speech of another person.
- Use fingers to grasp, move, or assemble very small objects.

It is not as important, but still necessary, for people in this career to be able to:

- See details of objects that are more than a few feet away.
- Use stomach and lower back muscles to support the body for long periods without getting tired.
- Focus on one source of sound and ignore others.
- Hear sounds and recognize the difference between them.
- See differences between colours, shades and brightness.
- Hold the arm and hand in one position or hold the hand steady while moving the arm.
- Use one or two hands to grasp, move, or assemble objects.

Skills and Abilities: People in this career need to:

Communicate

- Listen to others, understand and ask questions.
- Express ideas clearly when speaking or writing.
- Read and understand written information.

Reason and Problem Solve

- Notice when something is wrong or is likely to go wrong.
- Analyze ideas and use logic to determine their strengths and weaknesses.
- Combine several pieces of information and draw conclusions.
- Develop rules or follow guidelines for arranging items.
- Think of new ideas or original and creative ways to solve problems.
- Use reasoning to discover answers to problems.
- Understand new information or materials by studying and working with them.
- Concentrate and not be distracted while performing a task.

Use Math and Science:

- Add, subtract, multiply and divide quickly and correctly.
- Use math skills to solve problems.

Manage Oneself, People, Time and Things:

- Go back and forth between two or more activities or sources of information without becoming confused.
- Check how well one is learning or doing something.

Work with People:

- Look for ways to help people.
- Be aware of others¿ reactions and change behaviour in relation to them.
- Use several methods to teach others how to do something.

Perceive and Visualize:

- Identify a pattern (a figure, object, word, or sound) that is hidden in distracting material.

Knowledge: People in this career need knowledge in the following areas:

- Customer and Personal Service: Knowledge of providing special services to customers based on their needs.
- Administration and Management: Knowledge of managing the operations of a business, company, or group.

- Clerical: Knowledge of general office work such as filing and recording information.
- English Language: Knowledge of the meaning, spelling and use of the English language.
- Mathematics: Knowledge of the rules and uses of numbers. Areas of knowledge include arithmetic, algebra, geometry and statistics.
- Sales and Marketing: Knowledge of advertising and selling products and services.

Interests: People in this career are people who tend to:

- Consider relationships important. They like to work in a friendly, non-competitive environment. They like to do things for other people. They prefer jobs where they are not pressured to do things that go against their sense of right and wrong.
- Consider support from their employer important. They like to be treated fairly and have supervisors who will back them up. They prefer jobs where they are trained well.
- Consider good working conditions important. They like jobs offering steady employment and good pay. They want employment that fits their individual work style. They may prefer doing a variety of tasks, working alone, or being busy all the time.
- Have conventional interests. They like work activities that follow set procedures, routines and standards. They like to work with data and detail. They prefer working where there is a clear line of authority to follow.
- Have enterprising interests. They like work activities that involve starting up and carrying out projects, especially in business. They like to lead and persuade others, make decisions and take risks for profit.
- Have social interests. They like work activities that assist others and promote learning and personal development. They like to communicate with others: to teach, give advice, help, or otherwise be of service to others.

Preparation: To work as a hotel desk clerk, you must: complete a high school diploma or GED; and complete on-the-job training.

On-the-job Training: Hotel desk clerks learn their skills on the job. A high school degree or GED is the most common educational requirement. Experience with computers is also helpful.

Orientation for hotel desk clerks usually includes an explanation of the job duties. You also receive information about the hotel and its services. You learn your tasks with help from a supervisor or experienced clerk. You also may receive special training on the hotel's computerized reservation and billing system. Training lasts about a month.

Outlook: In Minnesota, the number of jobs for hotel desk clerks is expected to grow faster than average through the year 2014. Nationally, the number of jobs for hotel desk clerks is expected to grow as fast as average through the year 2014.

Much of the increase in jobs will come from the expected increase in business and leisure travel. The hotel and motel industry is changing and more luxury hotels are being built. These hotels have more staff and desk clerks can spend a lot of time taking care of guest's needs.

Automation will slightly reduce the need for hotel desk clerks. Some hotels and motels allow guests to check out by phone or television instead of going to the front desk. As some of their more traditional duties are automated, however, many desk clerks are assuming a wider range of responsibilities.

Employment of hotel desk clerks is affected by the economy. When the economy slows down, travel declines and hotels need fewer desk clerks. Depending on the location of the property, work may be seasonal.

	Employment	*Employment Change*		
	2002	2012	Number	Percent
National	195,300	228,900	33,600	17.2

Advancement Opportunities: Experienced hotel desk clerks can advance by transferring to a job with more responsibility or by becoming a supervisor. They can improve their chances for advancement by taking courses in hospitality management.

Janitor and Housekeeper Supervisors

Overview: Janitor and housekeeper supervisors oversee the work of cleaning staff.

"An uncluttered home means an uncluttered mind." Or so the saying goes. You can easily interchange the words "desk", "office," even "building" for home and the meaning is still clear: to function well, you must keep your space clean. That's why the services of janitors and housekeepers are so important. So important, in fact, that the management of the Empire State Building employs them to clean and straighten the building's offices on a nightly basis. In addition, they work with supervisors to make sure that walls, windows, floors and drapes are regularly deep-cleaned. Janitors and housekeepers clean buildings and keep them in good shape. They work in office buildings, stores, hospitals, hotels, schools and other types of buildings. Janitor and housekeeping supervisors schedule and supervise these workers.

Supervisors assign duties to janitors and cleaners. They inspect their work to be sure it meets standards of cleanliness. Supervisors take inventory to be sure they have enough supplies. They also issue cleaning supplies and equipment to workers. Equipment depends on the building being cleaned and the tasks assigned. For example, one job may require a mop and a bucket. Another job may require an electric polishing machine and a special cleaning solution. Supervisors make sure the equipment is in proper working order and may maintain and fix them.

Janitor and housekeeper supervisors interview job applicants and hire new workers. They also recommend that staff be promoted or fired. Supervisors attend company staff meetings to discuss policies or customers¿ complaints. In addition, supervisors train new and experienced workers. They explain policies and work procedures. They may set up standards and procedures of their own. They also show staff how to use and maintain the equipment.

Supervisors record employee data, such as tasks assigned or hours worked. They also prepare reports on payroll and expenses. In addition, some supervisors have cleaning duties.

Other titles and keywords for this career.

Work Activities: The following list of occupational tasks is specific to this career.

- Schedule and supervise the work of janitors and housekeepers.
- Assign tasks and inspect work to be sure it meets cleanliness standards.
- Issue supplies and equipment to workers.
- Inventory stock of cleaning supplies and order items. Check equipment to make sure it is working properly.
- Interview job applicants, hire staff and recommend promotions and dismissals.
- Attend staff meetings to discuss company policies and customers' complaints.
- Establish standards and procedures for housekeeping staff. Investigate complaints.
- Train new and experienced workers in policies, procedures and use of equipment.
- Record employee data and prepare reports.
- May perform cleaning duties.
- If working in hospitals or clinics, ensure germs and infections aren't spread.
- If working in hotels, work with manager to resolve conflicts and notify them when rooms are ready.

People in this career perform the following list of tasks, but the tasks are common to many occupations.

- Get information needed to do the job.
- Coordinate the work and activities of others.
- Inspect equipment, structures, or materials.
- Identify objects, actions and events.
- Make decisions and solve problems.
- Judge the value of objects, services, or people.

- Resolve conflicts and negotiate with others.
- Schedule work and activities.

Working Conditions: In a typical work setting, people in this career:

Interpersonal Relationships:

- Have a high level of social contact. They work closely with those they supervise.
- Communicate daily by telephone, face-to-face discussions and e-mail.
- Are responsible for the work outcomes and results of other workers.
- Are responsible for the health and safety of their workers and their clients.
- May be placed in conflict situations in which others may become angry or rude.
- Often work as part of a team.

Physical Work Conditions:

- Often work indoors, but may work outdoors for brief periods.
- Are sometimes exposed to contaminants such as cleaning solutions.
- Frequently wear safety attire, such as masks, to protect them from fumes.
- May be exposed to diseases or infections from soiled client items.
- May work physically close to others, usually a few feet away.

Work Performance:

- Must be sure that all details are done and their work is exact so that clients are happy with their work.
- Make most decisions and set their daily tasks and goals without consulting another first.
- Must meet daily and weekly deadlines.

Hours/Travel:

- Usually work a 40-hour week. Schedules are usually regular and established.

- Often work evenings and weekends, when buildings are empty.

Physical Demands: People in this career frequently:

- Stand when overseeing workers.
- Walk between work sites.
- Use hands to handle, control, or feel objects, tools, or controls.

It is not as important, but still necessary, for people in this career to be able to:

- Speak clearly so listeners can understand.
- See details of objects whether they are nearby or far away.
- Use stomach and lower back muscles to support the body for long periods without getting tired.
- Understand the speech of another person.

Skills and Abilities: People in this career need to:

Communicate

- Express ideas clearly when speaking or writing.
- Read and understand work-related materials.
- Listen to others, understand and ask questions.

Reason and Problem Solve:

- Understand new information or materials by studying and working with them.
- Analyze ideas and use logic to determine their strengths and weaknesses.
- Judge the costs and benefits of a possible action.
- Identify problems and review information. Develop, review and apply solutions.

Use Math and Science:

- Use math skills to solve problems.

Manage Oneself, People, Time and Things:

- Check how well one is learning or doing something.
- Manage the time of self and others.
- Motivate, develop and direct people as they work.

Work with People:

- Teach others how to do something, using several methods.
- Be aware of others¿ reactions and change behaviour in relation to them.
- Look for ways to help people.
- Persuade others to approach things differently.
- Solve problems by bringing others together to discuss differences.

Work with Things:

- Determine the tools and equipment needed to do a job.
- Operate and control equipment.
- Maintain equipment on a routine basis. Determine when and what kind of maintenance is needed.

Knowledge: People in this career need knowledge in the following areas:

- Mechanical: Knowledge of designing, using and repairing machines and tools.
- Administration and Management: Knowledge of managing the operations of a business, company, or group.
- Customer and Personal Service: Knowledge of providing special services to customers based on their needs.
- Psychology: Knowledge of people, their actions and mental processes. This may include knowledge of how to treat emotional and behavioural problems.
- Public Safety and Security: Knowledge of protecting people, data and property.
- Chemistry: Knowledge of the properties of substances and the changes that occur when they interact.
- Production and Processing: Knowledge of how products are made and supplied.
- Building and Construction: Knowledge of constructing buildings and other structures.

Interests: People in this career are people who tend to:

- Consider relationships important. They like to work in a friendly, non-competitive environment. They like to do things for other people. They prefer jobs where they are not pressured to do things that go against their sense of right and wrong.

- Consider independence important. They like to make decisions and try out ideas on their own. They prefer jobs where they can plan their work with little supervision.
- Consider good working conditions important. They like jobs offering steady employment and good pay. They want employment that fits their individual work style. They may prefer doing a variety of tasks, working alone, or being busy all the time.
- Consider achievement important. They like to see the results of their work and to use their strongest abilities. They like to get a feeling of accomplishment from their work.
- Have enterprising interests. They like work activities that involve starting up and carrying out projects, especially in business. They like to lead and persuade others, make decisions and take risks for profit.
- Have conventional interests. They like work activities that follow set procedures, routines and standards. They like to work with data and detail. They prefer working where there is a clear line of authority to follow.
- Have realistic interests. They like work activities that include practical, hands-on problems and solutions. They like to work with plants, animals and physical materials such as wood, tools and machinery. They often prefer to work outside.

Preparation: To work as a janitor and housekeeping supervisor, you must: have a high school diploma or GED; have work experience; and have good interpersonal skills.

Work Experience: Janitor and housekeeping supervisors usually have many years of experience working as a janitor or housekeeper. This allows them to move up in their field.

On-the-job Training: In some cases, employers will offer some training to new supervisors. This will depend on the employer.

Outlook: In Minnesota, the number of jobs for janitor and housekeeper supervisors is expected to grow faster than average through the year 2014.

Nationally, the number of jobs for janitor and housekeeper supervisors is expected to grow faster than average through the year 2014.

The number of office buildings, hotels, schools and other buildings is increasing. Most of these buildings will need janitors and housekeepers to clean them. This will increase the need for supervisors. Businesses that provide janitorial and cleaning services on a contract basis will also grow. Many firms try to reduce costs by contracting for these services rather than hiring their own workers.

	Employment	*Employment Change*		
	2002	2012	Number	Percent
National	235,900	280,600	44,700	18.9

Advancement Opportunities: Advancement for janitors is limited in organizations where they are the only maintenance worker. However, in organizations where there is a large maintenance staff, experienced janitors and cleaners can become supervisors. A high school diploma or GED improves the chances of advancement.

Supervisors usually move up through the ranks as they gain experience. In many jobs, they are required to take some in-service training to improve their supervisory skills. A four-year college degree is required in some settings. Any education improves advancement opportunities.

Maids and Housekeepers

Overview: Maids and housekeepers clean rooms at hotels, motels and hospitals.

The philosopher Friedrich Nietzsche once said, "A man with genius is unendurable if he does not also possess at least two other things: gratitude and cleanliness." While Nietzsche may have meant something more lofty than a sparkling bathroom, most people agree that cleanliness is indeed next to godliness - or pretty close. That goes double for hotel rooms.

Imagine walking into a room for the first time and finding the bed unmade!

Thankfully, maids and housekeepers keep guest rooms clean and tidy. Most maids and housekeepers work at hotels, motels and resorts. They clean guest rooms, meeting rooms, restrooms and common areas such as lobbies. They vacuum carpets and sweep, wash and wax floors. Maids and housekeepers also dust furniture, polish metalwork and replace light bulbs. Occasionally they wash walls, windows and woodwork. In addition, they empty trash cans and carry the garbage to dumpsters. In guest rooms, maids and housekeepers remove used linens and towels. They remake beds and replace items the previous guests used, such as soaps and drinking glasses. Besides cleaning, they may deliver cribs, ironing boards and rollaway beds to guest rooms. They may also help set up for weddings or business meetings. Larger hotels usually hire more staff. At those hotels, maids and housekeepers may be limited to cleaning rooms.

In hospitals, maids and housekeepers use solutions that kill germs to disinfect equipment. They brush mattresses and wash bed frames. Like maids in hotels, they make beds and restock items, such as tissues. Maids and housekeepers need to know how to use various types of cleaning supplies and equipment. They also need to know how to use cleaning solutions safely so they do not harm themselves or others. Maids and housekeepers also clean office buildings, residence halls and health clubs. No matter where they work, they must use safety precautions to protect their guests and themselves. Especially at large hotels and resorts, they must also be on guard against theft and damage.

Some housekeepers may work for private clients at their homes. Their duties may also include caring for children or elderly people from time to time. They may do light cooking and run errands, depending on the needs of the client.

Other titles and keywords for this career.

Work Activities: The following list of occupational tasks is specific to this career.

- Remove used linens and towels. Remake beds.

- Vacuum carpets. Sweep, wash and wax floors.
- Dust furniture, polish fixtures and replace light bulbs.
- Wash walls, windows, mirrors and woodwork.
- Collect used items and replace with clean ones, such as soaps and drinking glasses.
- Empty wastebaskets and ash trays. Carry trash out for pickup.
- Deliver ironing boards, baby cribs and rollaway beds to guests' rooms.
- Prepare rooms for meetings or social events.
- Wash bed frames and brush mattresses.
- Use various tools and cleaners.
- Use wheeled carts to carry supplies and soiled items.
- Observe safety and other precautions to protect property and report theft.
- May run errands and care for children and elderly persons, depending on the type of job and location.

People in this career perform the following list of tasks, but the tasks are common to many occupations.

- Get information needed to do the job.
- Perform activities that use the whole body.
- Establish and maintain relationships.

Working Conditions: In a typical work setting, people in this career:

Interpersonal Relationships:

- Are responsible for the health and safety of clients and guests. Good cleaning ensures sanitary conditions.
- Have a low to medium level of social contact. They talk to guests and supervisors, but spend most of their time alone.
- Are somewhat responsible for the work done by other maids and housekeepers.
- Communicate mostly by face-to-face discussions.
- May work as part of a team.

Physical Work Conditions:

- Usually work indoors when cleaning. They rarely work outdoors. In some cases, they may be outdoors when walking from room to room.
- Sometimes wear a special uniform. This depends on the company they work for and if they interact with the public.
- Are regularly exposed to contaminants and diseases or infections. They work with cleaning chemicals and clean soiled items.
- Make work physically near other maids and housekeepers, such as when cleaning the same hotel room.

Work Performance:

- Must fully complete and be exact in their work. If rooms are not clean, guests may not return in the future.
- Repeat the same tasks.
- Usually make decisions and set daily tasks and goals under the guidance of a supervisor.
- Must meet daily and weekly deadlines.

Hours/Travel:

- May work part time or full time. Schedules are typically established.
- May work days, evenings, or weekends.

Physical Demands: People in this career frequently:

- Walk around rooms while cleaning them.
- Stand for long periods of time.
- Bend or twist their body.
- Repeat the same motions.
- Use hands to handle, control, or feel objects, tools, or controls.
- Kneel, stoop, crouch, or crawl.

It is important for people in this career to be able to:

- Bend, stretch, twist, or reach out.

It is not as important, but still necessary, for people in this career to be able to:

- See details of objects whether they are nearby or far away.
- Understand the speech of another person.
- Speak clearly so listeners can understand.
- Use stomach and lower back muscles to support the body for long periods without getting tired.
- Hold the arm and hand in one position or hold the hand steady while moving the arm.
- Coordinate movement of several parts of the body, such as arms and legs, while the body is moving.
- Use fingers and hands to grasp, move, or assemble very small objects.
- Be physically active for long periods without getting tired or out of breath.
- Move two or more limbs together (for example, two arms, two legs, or one leg and one arm) while remaining in place.
- Use muscles to lift, push, pull, or carry heavy objects.
- See differences between colours, shades and brightness.
- Use muscles for extended periods without getting tired.
- Move arms and legs quickly.

Skills and Abilities: People in this career need to:

Communicate

- Understand spoken information.
- Read and understand work-related materials.

Manage Oneself, People, Time and Things:

- Manage the time of self and others.

Work with Things:

- Operate and control equipment.

Knowledge: People in this career need knowledge in the following areas:

- Customer and Personal Service: Knowledge of providing special services to customers based on their needs.

Interests: People in this career are people who tend to:

- Consider relationships important. They like to work in a friendly, non-competitive environment. They like to do things for other people. They prefer jobs where they are not pressured to do things that go against their sense of right and wrong.
- Have realistic interests. They like work activities that include practical, hands-on problems and solutions. They like to work with plants, animals and physical materials such as wood, tools and machinery. They often prefer to work outside.
- Have conventional interests. They like work activities that follow set procedures, routines and standards. They like to work with data and detail. They prefer working where there is a clear line of authority to follow.
- Have social interests. They like work activities that assist others and promote learning and personal development. They like to communicate with others: to teach, give advice, help, or otherwise be of service to others.

Preparation: To work as a maid or housekeeper, you must: complete on-the-job training; and be self-motivated.

Formal Education: No formal training is required beyond high school. In some cities, unions or government agencies offer training programmes. In these programmes you learn how to select and use cleaning products. You also learn to operate machines such as buffers, polishers and vacuums. In addition, you study safety and health regulations and learn how to work without supervision.

On-the-job Training: Most maids and housekeepers learn their skills on the job from an experienced worker. During training, you start with routine cleaning jobs and learn more complex tasks and you gain experience. Training usually lasts a month.

Outlook: In Minnesota, the number of jobs for maids and housekeepers is expected to grow about as fast as average through the year 2014.

Nationally, the number of jobs for maids and housekeepers is expected to grow as fast as average through the year 2014.

The number of hotels, motels and hospitals built is expected to continue increasing. Additional maids and housekeepers will be needed to clean these facilities. The number of maids and housekeepers who work for private households is expected to decline. This is because many families are using home cleaning services for a few hours a week instead of keeping someone on staff.

Since this is such a large occupation, there will be many openings as maids or housekeepers switch jobs or retire from the field.

	Employment	*Employment Change*		
	2002	2012	Number	Percent
National	1,422,000	1,587,400	165,400	11.6

Advancement Opportunities: For maids and housekeepers, advancement often is in the form of higher pay. However, those who work for large organizations may move up in their company. Experienced maids and housekeepers can become supervisors. A high school diploma or GED increases a worker's chance of advancement.

Customer Service Representatives

Significant Points: Job prospects are expected to be excellent.

Most jobs require only a high school diploma but educational requirements are rising.

Strong verbal communication and listening skills are important.

Nature of the Work: Customer service representatives are employed by many different types of companies throughout the country to serve as a direct point of contact for customers. They are responsible for ensuring that their company's customers receive an adequate level of service or help with their questions and concerns. These customers may be individual consumers or other companies and the nature of their service needs can vary considerably.

All customer service representatives interact with customers to provide information in response to inquiries about products or services and to handle and resolve complaints. They communicate with customers through a variety of means—by telephone; by e-mail, fax, or regular mail correspondence; or in person. Some customer service representatives handle general questions and complaints, whereas others specialize in a particular area.

Many customer inquiries involve routine questions and requests. For example, customer service representatives may be asked to provide a customer with their credit card balance, or to check on the status of an order that has been placed. Obtaining the answers to such questions usually requires simply looking up information on their computer. Other questions are more involved and may call for additional research or further explanation on the part of the customer service representative. In handling customers' complaints, customer service representatives must attempt to resolve the problem according to guidelines established by the company. These procedures may involve asking questions to determine the validity of a complaint; offering possible solutions; or providing customers with refunds, exchanges, or other offers, such as discounts or coupons. In some cases, customer service representatives are required to follow up with an individual customer until a question is answered or an issue is resolved.

Some customer service representatives help people decide what types of products or services would best suit their needs. They may even aid customers in completing purchases or transactions. Although the primary function of customer service representatives is not sales, some may spend a part of their time with customers encouraging them to purchase additional products or services. (For information on workers whose primary function is sales). Customer service representatives also may make changes or updates to a customer's profile or account information. They may keep records of transactions and update and maintain databases of information.

Most customer service representatives use computers and telephones extensively in their work. Customer service representatives frequently enter information into a computer as they are speaking to customers. Often, companies have large amounts of data, such as account information, that can be pulled up on a computer screen while the representative is talking to a customer so that he or she can answer specific questions relating to the account. Customer service representatives also may have access to information such as answers to the most common customer questions, or guidelines for dealing with complaints.

In the event that they encounter a question or situation to which they do not know how to respond, workers consult with a supervisor to determine the best course of action. Customer service representatives use multiline telephones systems, which often route calls directly to the most appropriate representative. However, at times, the customer service representative must transfer a call to someone who may be better able to respond to the customer's needs.

In some organizations, customer service representatives spend their entire day on the telephone. In others, they may spend part of their day answering e-mails and the remainder of the day taking calls. For some, most of their contact with the customer is face to face. Customer service representatives need to remain aware of the amount of time spent with each customer so that they can fairly distribute their time among the people who require their assistance.

This is particularly important for customer service representatives whose primary activities are answering telephone calls and whose conversations often are required to be kept within set time limits. For customer service representatives working in call centres, there usually is very little time between telephone calls; as soon as representatives have finished with one call, they must move on to another. When working in call centres, customer service representatives are likely to be under close supervision. Telephone calls may be taped and reviewed by supervisors to ensure that company policies and procedures are being followed, or a supervisor may listen in on conversations.

Job responsibilities can differ, depending on the industry in which a customer service representative is employed. For example, a customer service representative working in the branch office of a bank may assume the responsibilities of other workers, such as teller or new account clerk, as needed. In insurance agencies, a customer service representative interacts with agents, insurance companies and policyholders. These workers handle much of the paperwork related to insurance policies, such as policy applications and changes and renewals to existing policies. They answer questions regarding policy coverage, help with reporting claims and do anything else that may need to be done.

Although they must know as much as insurance agents about insurance products and usually must have credentials equal to those of an agent in order to sell products and make changes to policies, the duties of a customer service representative differ from those of an agent in that customer service representatives are not responsible for actively seeking potential customers. Customer service representatives employed by utilities and communications companies assist individuals interested in opening accounts for various utilities such as electricity and gas, or for communication services such as cable television and telephone. They explain various options and receive orders for services to be installed, turned on, turned off, or changed. They also may look into and resolve complaints about billing and service provided by utility, telephone and cable television companies.

Working Conditions: Although customer service representatives can work in a variety of settings, most work in areas that are clean and well lit. Many work in call or customer contact centres. In this type of environment, workers generally have their own workstation or cubicle space equipped with a telephone, headset and computer. Because many call centres are open extended hours, beyond the traditional work day, or are staffed around the clock, these positions may require workers to take on early morning, evening, or late night shifts. Weekend or holiday work also may be necessary. As a result, the occupation is well suited to flexible work schedules. Nearly 1 out of 5 customer service representatives work part time. The occupation also offers the opportunity for seasonal work in certain industries, often through temporary help agencies.

Call centres may be crowded and noisy and work may be repetitious and stressful, with little time between calls. Workers usually must attempt to minimize the length of each call, while still providing excellent service. To ensure that these procedures are followed, conversations may be monitored by supervisors, something that can be stressful. Also, long periods spent sitting, typing, or looking at a computer screen may cause eye and muscle strain, backaches, headaches and repetitive motion injuries.

Customer service representatives working outside of a call center environment may interact with customers through several different means. For example, workers employed by an insurance agency or in a grocery store may have customers approach them in person or contact them by telephone, computer, mail, or fax. Many of these customer service representatives work a standard 40-hour week; however, their hours generally depend on the hours of operation of the establishment in which they are employed. Work environments outside of a call center also vary accordingly. Most customer service representatives work either in an office or at a service or help desk.

For virtually all types of customer service representatives, dealing with difficult or irate customers can be a trying task; however, the ability to resolve customers' problems has the potential to be very rewarding.

Training, Other Qualifications and Advancement: Most customer service representative jobs require only a high school diploma. However, due to employers demanding a higher skilled workforce, many customer service jobs now require an associate or bachelor's degree. Basic to intermediate computer knowledge and good interpersonal skills also are important qualities for people who wish to be successful in the field. Because customer service representatives constantly interact with the public, good communication and problem-solving skills are a must. Verbal communication and listening skills are especially important. Additionally, for workers who communicate through e-mail, good typing, spelling and written communication skills are necessary. High school courses in computers, English, or business are helpful in preparing for a job in customer service.

Customer service representatives play a critical role in providing an interface between customer and company and for this reason employers seek out people who come across in a friendly and professional manner. The ability to deal patiently with problems and complaints and to remain courteous when faced with difficult or angry people is very important. Also, a customer service representative needs to be able to work independently within specified time constraints. Workers should have a clear and pleasant speaking voice and be fluent in English. However, the ability to speak a foreign language is becoming increasingly necessary and bilingual skills are considered a plus.

Training requirements vary by industry. Almost all customer service representatives are provided with some training prior to beginning work and training continues once on the job. This training generally covers customer service and phone skills, products and services and common customer problems with them, the use or operation of the telephone and/or computer systems and company policies and regulations. Length of training varies, but it usually lasts at least several weeks. Because of a constant need to update skills and knowledge, most customer service representatives continue to receive instruction and training throughout their career. This is particularly true of workers in industries such as banking, in which regulations and products are continually changing.

Although some positions may require previous industry, office, or customer service experience, many customer service jobs are entry level. Customer service jobs are often good introductory positions into a company or an industry. In some cases, experienced workers can move up within the company into supervisory or managerial positions or they may move into areas such as product development, in which they can use their knowledge to improve products and services.

Within insurance agencies and brokerages, however, a customer service representative job usually is not an entry-level position. Workers must have previous experience in insurance and are often required by State regulations to be licensed like insurance sales agents. A variety of designations are available to demonstrate that a candidate has sufficient knowledge and skill and continuing education and training are often offered through the employer. As they gain more knowledge of industry products and services, customer service representatives in insurance may advance to other, higher level positions, such as insurance sales agent.

Employment: Customer service representatives held about 2.1 million jobs in 2004. Although they were found in a variety of industries, about 1 in 4 customer service representatives worked in finance and insurance. The largest numbers were employed by insurance carriers, insurance agencies and brokerages and banks and credit unions.

About 1 in 8 customer service representatives were employed in administrative and support services. These workers were concentrated in the business support services industry (which includes telephone call centres) and employment services (which includes temporary help services and employment placement agencies). Another 1 in 8 customer service representatives were employed in retail trade establishments such as general merchandise stores, food and beverage stores, or nonstore retailers. Other industries that employ significant numbers of customer service representatives include information, particularly the telecommunications industry; manufacturing, such as printing and related support activities; and wholesale trade.

Although they are found in all States, customer service representatives who work in call centres tend to be concentrated geographically. Four States—California, Texas, Florida and New York—employ 30 percent of customer service representatives. Delaware, Arizona, South Dakota and Utah, have the highest concentration of workers in this occupation, with customer service representatives comprising over 2 percent of total employment in these States.

Job Outlook: Prospects for obtaining a job in this field are expected to be excellent, with more job openings than jobseekers. Bilingual jobseekers, in particular, may enjoy favourable job prospects. In addition to many new openings occurring as businesses and organizations expand, numerous job openings will result from the need to replace experienced customer service representatives who transfer to other occupations or leave the labour force. Replacement needs are expected to be significant in this large occupation because many young people work as customer service representatives before switching to other jobs. This occupation is well suited to flexible work schedules and many opportunities for part-time work will continue to be available, particularly as organizations attempt to cut labour costs by hiring more temporary workers.

Employment of customer service representatives is expected to increase faster than the average for all occupations through the year 2014. Beyond growth stemming from expansion of the industries in which customer service representatives are employed, a need for additional customer service representatives is likely to result from heightened reliance on these workers. Customer service is critical to the success of any organization that deals with customers and strong customer service can build sales and visibility as companies try to distinguish themselves from competitors.

In many industries, gaining a competitive edge and retaining customers will be increasingly important over the next decade. This is particularly true in industries such as financial services, communications and utilities, which already employ numerous customer service representatives. As the trend toward consolidation in industries continues, centralized call centres will provide an effective method for delivering a high level of customer service. As a result, employment of customer service representatives may grow at a faster rate in call centres than in other areas. However, this growth may be tempered: a variety of factors, including technological improvements, make it increasingly feasible and cost-effective for call centres to be built or relocated outside of the United States.

Technology is affecting the occupation in many ways. The Internet and automated teller machines have provided customers with means of obtaining information and conducting transactions that do not entail interacting with another person. Technology also allows for a greater streamlining of processes, while at the same time increasing the productivity of workers. The use of computer software to filter e-mails, generating automatic responses or directing messages to the appropriate representative and the use of similar systems to answer or route telephone inquiries are likely to become more prevalent in the future. Also, with rapidly improving telecommunications, some organizations have begun to position their call centres overseas.

Despite such developments, the need for customer service representatives is expected to remain strong. In many ways, technology has heightened consumers' expectations for information and services and availability of information online seems to have generated more need for customer service representatives, particularly to respond to e-mail. Also, technology cannot replace human skills. As more sophisticated technologies are able to resolve many customers' questions and concerns, the nature of the inquiries to be handled by customer service representatives is likely to become increasingly complex.

Furthermore, the job responsibilities of customer service representatives are expanding. As companies downsize or take other measures to increase profitability, workers are being trained to perform additional duties such as opening bank accounts or cross-selling products. As a result, employers may increasingly prefer customer service representatives who have education beyond high school, such as some college or even a college degree. While jobs in some industries, such as retail trade, may be affected by economic downturns, the customer service occupation is generally resistant to major fluctuations in employment.

Earnings: In May 2004, median annual earnings for wage and salary customer service representatives were $27,020. The middle 50 percent earned between $21,510 and $34,560. The lowest 10 percent earned less than $17,680 and the highest 10 percent earned more than $44,160.

Earnings for customer service representatives vary according to level of skill required, experience, training, location and size of firm. Median annual earnings in the industries employing the largest numbers of these workers in May 2004 are shown below:

Insurance carriers	$29,790
Agencies, brokerages and other insurance related activities	28,800
Depository credit intermediation	26,140
Employment services	23,100
Business support services	21,390

In addition to receiving an hourly wage, full-time customer service representatives who work evenings, nights, weekends, or holidays may receive shift differential pay. Also, because call centres are often open during extended hours, or even 24 hours a day, some customer service representatives have the benefit of being able to work a schedule that does not conform to the traditional workweek. Other benefits can include life and health insurance, pensions, bonuses, employer-provided training and discounts on the products and services the company offers.

4

Career in Tourism Industry

The future predictions are that worldwide travel will continue to grow, creating more job opportunities than ever!

An estimated 255 million people worldwide are employed directly or indirectly in travel, tourism and hospitality-related jobs and the industry is expected to create 144 million more jobs in the coming years. Whatever ones ultimate career goal is, the continued growth of worldwide travel, for business or leisure, makes career opportunities overseas an exciting reality.

Career Opportunities: Career Options in the travel and tourism industry are varied and tremendous.

Tourism Department : Reservation & Counter staff, Sales and marketing staff and Tour Planners.

Airlines: Traffic Assistance, Reservation and Counter Staff, Airhostess and Flight Pursers, Sales and Marketing staff and Customer Services.

Travel Agencies : Reservation and Counter staff, Sales and Marketing staff, Tour Escorts and Tour Operators, Cargo and Courier Agencies etc.

Hotels : Operations Manager, Front Office, House Keeping, Food and Beverages, Accounting, Engineering/ Maintenance, Sales, Public Relations etc.

Travel and Tourism

With the recent developments in transportation and communication, travelling, both domestically and internationally has come to be unproblematic. Whether your purpose of travelling is business, adventure or just a vacation, a large group of people belonging to the Travel and Tourism industry are there to make your experience trouble free. This industry is the largest foreign exchange earner and it provides employment to millions of people. Hence the industry has a number of career options to offer and the scope of employment is unbounded.

Employment opportunities exist in both the public and the private sector in this industry. In the public sector, you can work in the Directorates and Departments of tourism of the center and the state, guides etc. In the private sector, on the other hand you can secure a job in a travel agency, hotel, airline, transport agency or a cargo company. Since this industry is a relatively new one, there are not a huge number of experienced individuals. Hence, you can move up the ladder fast and establish your own agency after a few years

The Career Options

Travel Agencies: These institutions facilitate travel and other services for all individuals travelling for vacations or business purposes. Providing information about the destination, hotel ratings, the cheapest and the fastest mode of transport, visas, foreign exchange etc. is the job of a travel agent. Travel agencies are divided into roughly four departments- the Accounts, Tours, Travel and Cargo. A course in travel and tourism will help you to get a suitable job.

Tourism Department: This department consists of reservation and counter staff, sales and marketing staff, tour planners, tour guides, information assistants and officers in the Directorate and Department of tourism. These officers for the Directorate and Department of tourism are chosen from the civil services and their job is to promote and plan tourism. Information assistants provide knowledge concerning destinations and plan itenaries. They are selected through a competitive exam which is held by the Staff Selection Commission. Guides too are divided into three categories namely regional, state and local. In order to be a guide, you must have knowledge about history, art, architecture and language.

Hotels: Hotels provide travellers with food and accommodation services. This service industry requires skilled and professional individuals and it's manpower requirements are vast. Jobs related to front office, operations, house keeping, food and beverages, accounting, management and public relations are available. A course in hotel management would help you to get a suitable job.

Transport: Transport refers to means of travelling from one place to another. Air, railways, road and sea are the basic categories that transport is divided into.

Road Transport: Coaches and tourist cars provide scope for self employment. Drivers with good conversation skills and knowledge of different languages are ideal for this job.

Airlines: This sector of the travel and tourism industry is in great demand. The ground staff and the airlines need smart and presentable professionals with a degree in hotel management or travel and tourism. Traffic assistants, reservation and counter staff, air hostess & flight pursuers, sales and marketing staff and people to provide customer services are all required. Airlines like Indian Airlines, Emirates, British Airways and Air India pay attractive salaries and provide a number of added benefits too.

Tour Operators: These individuals organize tours and manage travel and stay of their clients. They conduct tours to known tourist attractions and some of them help the tourists indulge in adventure sports like river rafting and rock climbing. To do this job, you have to have a pleasant personality, detailed knowledge concerning travel and language skills.

Time Share Companies: These companies own/manage holiday resorts with time shares owned by different members of these companies. It leads to another set of companies which provide services relating to sale/transfer/exchange of these time shares with an international network of resorts. You have the option of working with resort owning companies or time share exchange companies like RCI.

Holiday Consultants: This is a relatively new career option in the travel and tourism industry. These professionals provide all the information to their clients. They sell the holiday, plan the itenary, make the travel plan, book the tickets and provide all the other details which are required.

Banks: Banks require people to assist tourists and travellers on foreign exchange. Usually MBA professionals are preferred for this job. Banks help in hotel and ticket bookings also.

Personal Attributes

To be a part of this industry, you need to have a pleasant personality and detailed knowledge concerning travelling and tourist destinations. You need to have good communication and language skills. Business tactics and social etiquettes are requiremed. Lastly, the ability and patience to help and provide hospitality is a must.

Salaries: You can admit yourself to a travel and tourism course after your senior secondary examination [10+2] or after your graduation in any discipline. You can expect to find a job fairly soon. You can expect a beginning salary of Rs.3500 to Rs.4500. If you work as a service manager, you can expect a salary of about Rs.10000 to Rs.15000. If you start your career through an airline after a IATTA/UFTTA degree. You can expect to start with a salary of Rs.12000 to Rs.15000.

Tour Operators

Tourist Guides: The Travel Industry - Job Scenario

The travel and tourism industry which is the largest foreign exchange earner among all International industries, currently provides direct employment to millions of people, and indirectly covers possibly all areas of economic activity. Moreover, the number is likely to increase with massive plans for future expansion, creating a demand for skilled and trained Indian personnel in various spheres of the National & International Travel Industry.

The Recruiters look for the following attributes :

The Must Have's

- Good communication and presentation skills.
- Aptitude for figure work.

- An outgoing, friendly personality and ability to handle people.
- Verbal fluency & aptitude for languages.
- Organizing ability, decisions- making skills, Problem solving skills & Team work.
- Awareness of people, places and areas of interest.
- A passion for travel & willingness to work hard, long hours, on weekends and holidays.

Eligibility: International Employers prefer Travel Management Courses introduced by various Universities and Prestigious Institutes at the certificate, PG Diploma, Bachelor Degree, and Master's Degree level.

The technical skills required to work in these exciting industries are the same all round the world. The skills and knowledge gained from an Indian Travel Institute Travel College training course transfer easily across international borders.

Careers in Travel and Tourism

Careers in travel and tourism are some of the most fun and exciting careers available. Many of these careers offer free or discounted travel to far off destinations. These careers are great for individuals who like to experience new people, places, and activities.

One of the careers in travel and tourism that doesn't require travel, yet can still provide opportunities for travel, is a travel agent. Travel agents provide their clients with vacation packages. Working as a travel agent involves great administrative skills as well as customer service and sales.

Many careers in travel and tourism can be found with various cruise lines. Cruise lines hire a variety of different positions including entertainers, housekeepers, bartenders, chefs, waitresses, and other staff. These positions, while requiring hard work and skill, offer a variety of rewards that include travel to tourist destinations.

Other careers in travel and tourism include working at various resorts. These resorts may hire staff to work all year or they may hire staff seasonally. These resorts are varied an include ski resorts, ranches, and other resorts. Many of these resorts offer lodging and other activities free or at a discount.

Fancy restaurants, night clubs, and hotels in tourist hot spots and also offer a variety of careers in travel and tourism related fields. Hotels hire housekeepers, waitresses, bell hops, front desk, valet and other staff. Night clubs may hire bouncers, bartenders, and entertainers. Restaurants may hire chefs, waitresses, hosts, and entertainers.

Other fun careers in travel and tourism include working at amusement parks, museums, and other fun tourist spots. Work at these centers may include working in stores, restaurants, and ticket booths. It can also hire entertainers, artists, game workers, ride runners, security, and other positions. The positions may give workers access to the organization free of charge and other benefits.

Careers at Tourism Whistler

Working at Tourism Whistler: Whistler's success is based on both its national and international appeal. Its recognition as a world-class resort is the result of strategic and aggressive marketing by Tourism Whistler employees and our members.

In the past few years, residents and tourists alike have witnessed the rapid growth and change in Whistler. New businesses, accommodation facilities, and first-class recreational facilities have sprung up to meet the growing needs of Whistler as a four-season resort. Employees of Tourism Whistler, are able to experience first hand the excitement of the resort while playing a key role in its ongoing development.

Tourism Whistler Culture: Our role is to drive the tourism industry in Whistler while generating business to our members. They look to us for results. Our culture fosters an environment that strives to create a positive and fulfilling experience for our staff while constantly delivering results for our members.

We seek people who are committed to our team, resort, organization, purpose and vision with passion and energy. As a member driven organization, through anticipating trends, optimizing resources and focusing our efforts and performance, we focus on achievement. A final cornerstone of our culture is respect, for our people, our partners and our environment.

If the above described work environment is one in which you feel you would thrive, we want to hear from you.

Tourism Education Activity

What is It?: The National Tourism Recruitment and Retention Partnership.

A new partnership initiative has been formally agreed between Scottish Enterprise, Careers Scotland and Springboard Scotland to help the tourism and hospitality sector improve skills, recruitment and retention. Careers Scotland staff, both locally and nationally, will be working closely with Scottish Enterprise, Springboard Scotland, Local Enterprise Companies, Future Skills Scotland, Jobcentre Plus and People 1st.

Careers Scotland will take the lead working with the education sector to deliver a range of activities, opportunities and events to enhance the promotion of jobs and careers in tourism and hospitality across different labour pools.

Springboard Scotland will work with the business world to deliver on behalf of the Partnership a major national industry conference, workshops for employers, a resource pack, a recruitment toolkit, local recruitment projects, place people into jobs and produce recruitment and retention plans.

Who is it Aimed At?: The activities and events will be based upon Careers Scotland's current range of products, suitably adapted to the tourism and hospitality profession and the local markets in which the Local/Regional Partnerships will operate.

The events will be aimed at young people in schools and colleges, and through key influencers such as parents, carers and teachers. The business community will be invited to participate helping to build strong school and business links and helping the pupils and students to improve their understanding of the world of work.

What are the Benefits?: The Partnerships will provide a more cohesive approach to helping individuals to realise the potential of a career in the tourism and hospitality sector, and pupils and students will learn through experiential learning, to build the confidence and enterprising positive attitudes that they need in order to become effective employees or entrepreneurs in the future.

Which area is this available in?

All Scottish Enterprise Areas.

Is staff training required?

Information sessions as part of team meetings. Opportunities to participate in events and activities as part of multi-disciplinary teams.

- assessing the impact that any planned developments may have upon the local environment weighed against of course the potential benefits.
- working very closely with businesses in attracting holiday makers, tour operators, restaurants and guest-houses, to build a picture of how effective existing policies are and what may need addressing in the future. An important part of the work is seeking to attract exhibitions and conferences to the area.
- overseeing the council's tourist information offices;
- operating their marketing and development activities within a set budget. (This financial aspect may also include the need to look for outside assistance – advertising or sponsorship support, for example.)

Skills and Interests: Good communication skills are essential in this line of work, as are marketing and promotional experience and skills. Also need is the ability to be creative, and write 'snappy' copy to promote the area and various events.

Excellent organisational skills and the ability to get on with a wide cross-section of people from business leaders, councillors, to residents and visitors are further required.

Entry Requirements: For new entrants, BTEC/SQA offers Higher National Diploma in business studies (tourism), a degree in travel and tourism or in business studies with an option in tourism, or a degree in a non-vocational subject plus a postgraduate diploma in sales and marketing. S/NVQs in Tourist Information at Levels 2-3 are available. Experience of travel and tourism industry is always useful.

Estimated Salary Range: Around £10,278 - £20,000 depending on the responsibilities of the job.

Please note that salary information is a guide only and there may be local agreements in place. For further information about salaries for particular positions, please contact your local council directly.

Future Prospects and Opportunities: Although a relatively new area within local government, tourism is a fast-growing and important aspect of its work. Entry is usually as an assistant tourism officer – leading to managerial positions. Promotion to more senior posts often requires officers moving to a different council.

According to the estimates published by the World Tourism Organisation, the tourism industry is one of the largest industries worldwide and provides direct employment to 19 million people and generates indirect employment for 38 million persons. The overall value added employment in the tourism sector including hotels and restaurants has been estimated to be 80,000 crores.

Four sectors of tourism industry:

- Central Government and State Government level—Directorates & Development Corporations, ITDC hotels, Immigration and customs services.
- Commercial sector—Transport and Travel Services through agencies
- Institutional sector—Hotels
- Services sector—Interpreters, tourist guide, sales and publicity

Travel Jobs

Tourism industry has achieved a fast growth rate to emerge as the major driving force of the global economy. On the basis of growth rate, India has been ranked the second, with Montenegro and China on the first and third position respectively. Over the next ten years, India is all set to gain an annual growth rate of 8.8 percent in the travel sales sector. This immense growth in travel and tourism industry has created plenty of job opportunities for hospitality and travel sales jobs in India.

Career Scopes: A person willing to make a career in hospitality jobs should look for openings in the avenues such as Tourism Department, Travel Agencies, Hotels, Road and Airlines Transport, Tour Operators, Time Share Companies, Holiday Consultants and Banks.

Eligibility: To get admitted in hospitality and travel sales courses, one should be a higher secondary pass. One can also pursue the courses through correspondence courses. Candidates proficient in at least one foreign language are preferred.

Education: Institutes certified under the Ministry of Culture and Tourism and other professional institutes offer degree and diploma programs. Some of the reputed institutes are:

- National Council for Hotel Management, Catering Technology and Applied Nutrition, Delhi
- Institute of Hotel Management, Aurangabad
- International Institute of Hotel Management, Kolkata

Remuneration: Job in hospitality and travel sales offers attractive pay packets. Salary scales often vary within the industry.

Travel Agents

Significant Points: Travel benefits, such as reduced rates for transportation and lodging, attract many people to this occupation.

Training at a postsecondary vocational school, college, or university is increasingly important. Travel agents increasingly specialize in specific destinations or type of travel or traveller.

Keen competition for jobs is expected.

Nature of the Work: Constantly changing airfares and schedules, thousands of available vacation packages and a vast amount of travel information on the Internet can make travel planning frustrating and time consuming. To sort out the many travel options, tourists and business people often turn to travel agents, who assess their needs and help them make the best possible travel arrangements. Also, many major cruise lines, resorts and specialty travel groups use travel agents to promote travel packages to millions of people every year.

In general, travel agents give advice on destinations and make arrangements for transportation, hotel accommodations, car rentals, tours and recreation. They also may advise on weather conditions, restaurants and tourist attractions. For international travel, agents also provide information on customs regulations, required papers (passports, visas and certificates of vaccination) and currency exchange rates.

Travel agents consult a variety of published and computer-based sources for information on departure and arrival times, fares and hotel ratings and accommodations. They may visit hotels, resorts and restaurants to evaluate comfort, cleanliness and quality of food and service so that they can base recommendations on their own travel experiences or those of colleagues or clients.

Travel agents also promote their services, using telemarketing, direct mail and the Internet. They make presentations to social and special-interest groups, arrange advertising displays and suggest company-sponsored trips to business managers. Travel agents no longer receive commission payments from domestic airlines and agents face increasing competition from the Internet for low-cost fares. In an effort to find a niche in the market, many travel agents now specialize in travel to certain regions or for certain groups of people, such as honeymooners, grandparents, or ethnic groups.

Working Conditions: Travel agents spend most of their time behind a desk conferring with clients, completing paperwork, contacting airlines and hotels for travel arrangements and promoting group tours. During vacation seasons and holiday periods, they may be under a great deal of pressure. Many agents, especially those who are self-employed, frequently work long hours. With advanced computer systems and telecommunication networks, it is increasingly common for travel agents to work at home.

Training, Other Qualifications and Advancement: The minimum requirement for those interested in becoming a travel agent is a high school diploma or equivalent. Technology and computerization have increased the training needs, however and many employers prefer applicants with more education, such as a postsecondary vocational award. Many vocational schools offer full-time travel agent programmes that last several months, as well as evening and weekend programmes.

Travel agent courses also are offered in public adult education programmes and in community and 4-year colleges. A few colleges offer bachelor's or master's degrees in travel and tourism. Although few college courses relate directly to travel or tourism, a college education sometimes is desired by employers to establish a background in fields such as computer science, geography, communication, foreign languages and world history. Courses in accounting and business management also are important, especially for those who expect to manage or start their own travel agencies.

The American Society of Travel Agents offers a correspondence course that provides a basic understanding of the travel industry. Travel agencies also provide on-the-job training for their employees, a significant part of which consists of computer instruction. All employers require computer skills of workers whose jobs involve the operation of airline and centralized reservation systems.

Continuing education is critical, as the abundance of travel information readily available through the Internet and other sources has resulted in a more informed consumer who wants to deal with an expert when choosing a travel agent. Experienced travel agents can take advanced self-study or group-study courses from the Travel Institute, leading to the Certified Travel Counsellor designation. The Travel Institute also offers marketing and sales skills development programmes and destination specialist programmes, which provide detailed knowledge of regions such as North America, Western Europe, the Caribbean and the Pacific Rim. With the trend toward more specialization, these and other destination specialist courses are increasingly important.

Personal travel experience or experience as an airline reservation agent is an asset because knowledge about a city or foreign country often helps influence a client's travel plans. Patience and the ability to gain the confidence of clients also are useful qualities. Travel agents must be well-organized, accurate and meticulous to compile information from various sources and plan and organize their clients' travel itineraries. Also, agents who specialize in business travel must work quickly and efficiently because business travel often must be arranged on short notice. As the Internet has become an important tool for making travel arrangements, more travel agencies are using websites to provide their services to clients. This trend has increased the importance of computer skills in this occupation. Other desirable qualifications include good writing and interpersonal and sales skills.

Some employees start as reservation clerks or receptionists in travel agencies. With experience and some formal training, they can take on greater responsibilities and eventually assume travel agent duties. In agencies with many offices, travel agents may advance to office manager or to other managerial positions.

Those who start their own agencies generally have had experience in an established agency. Before they can receive commissions, these agents usually must gain formal approval from suppliers or corporations, such as airlines, ship lines, or rail lines. The Airlines Reporting Corporation and the International Airlines Travel Agency Network, for example, are the approving bodies for airlines. To gain approval, an agency must be financially sound and employ at least one experienced manager or travel agent.

There are no Federal licensing requirements for travel agents. In 2004, however, 13 States required some form of registration or certification of retail sellers of travel services.

Employment: Travel agents held about 103,000 jobs in 2004 and are found in every part of the country. More than

3 out of 5 agents worked for travel agencies. Around 14 percent were self-employed.

Job Outlook: Employment of travel agents is expected to decline through 2014. Most openings will occur as experienced agents transfer to other occupations or leave the labour force. Because of the projected decline in employment and the fact that a number of people are attracted by the travel benefits associated with this occupation, keen competition for jobs is expected. Travel agents who specialize and can utilize the Internet to reduce their costs and better compete with other travel suppliers should have the best chance for success.

The Internet increasingly allows people to access travel information from their personal computers, enabling them to research and plan their own trips, make their own reservations and travel arrangements and purchase their own tickets. As a result, demand will decline for travel agents who simply take orders, such as booking tickets for a specified date and time. Also, domestic airlines no longer pay commissions to travel agencies, which has reduced revenues and caused some agencies to go out of business.

This change also has led many travel agents to begin charging fees for their services. To justify those fees, customers expect travel agents to provide good service and travel expertise. Opportunities may be better for agents who specialize in specific destinations, luxury travel, or particular types of travellers such as ethnic groups or groups with a special interest or hobby.

Many consumers still prefer to use a professional travel agent to plan a complete trip; to deal with some of the more complex transactions; to ensure reliability; to suggest excursions or destinations that might otherwise be missed; to save time; or, in some cases, to save money.

Several factors should offset the adverse effect of Internet travel arrangement and the loss of revenues from airline bookings. For example, spending on tourism and travel is expected to increase over the next decade. With rising household incomes, smaller families and an increasing number of older people who are more likely to travel, more people are expected to travel on vacation—and to do so more frequently—than in the past.

Business travel also should rebound from recession and terrorism-related declines as business activity expands. Business travel also should increase as US businesses open more foreign operations and businesses increasingly sell their goods and services worldwide. In addition, luxury and specialty travel should increase among the growing number of Americans with the available time and money for these more expensive trips.

Another positive factor is the increasing affordability of air travel. Greater competition among airlines, especially from low-cost carriers, has brought airfares within the budgets of more people. In addition, American travel agents now organize more tours for the growing number of foreign visitors. Also, travel agents often are able to offer various travel packages at a substantial discount.

The demand for travel is sensitive to economic downturns and international political crises, when travel plans are likely to be deferred. Therefore, the number of job opportunities for travel agents fluctuates. However, the number of travellers has risen recently, possibly reflecting demand from consumers who delayed travel because of terrorism and safety concerns. Demand for travel remains volatile, though and trends could change at any time.

Earnings: Experience, sales ability and the size and location of the agency determine the salary of a travel agent. Median annual earnings of travel agents were $27,640 in May 2004. The middle 50 percent earned between $21,600 and $35,070. The lowest 10 percent earned less than $17,180, while the top 10 percent earned more than $44,090. Median earnings in May 2004 for travel agents employed in the travel arrangement and reservation services industry were $27,490.

Salaried agents usually enjoy standard employer-paid benefits that self-employed agents must provide for themselves. When travelling for personal reasons, agents usually get reduced rates for transportation and accommodations. In addition, agents sometimes take "familiarization" trips, at lower cost or no cost to themselves, to learn about various vacation sites. These benefits attract many people to this occupation.

Earnings of travel agents who own their agencies depend mainly on commissions from travel-related bookings and service fees they charge clients. Often it takes time to acquire a sufficient number of clients to have adequate earnings, so it is not unusual for new self-employed agents to have low earnings. Established agents may have lower earnings during economic downturns.

Overview: Travel agents plan trips and make travel arrangements for their clients.

You've saved for years and you finally have enough money for your dream vacation. You want to go overseas and spend at least two weeks trekking through ancient ruins, bustling cities and famous museums. You find out that it's not a good time to go in August, but wait ¿ that's when you planned to go. Oh! you do need a passport after all. And there are two large cities you can fly into, but you only knew about one. You scratch your head. It's a lot of work to plan your vacation! This could be the time to call a travel agent and get help.

Travel agents talk to customers to find out more about their travel plans. They learn where customers want to go, when they want to travel and what their budget is. Then they use computers to look up flight, cruise, hotel and car rental information. For example, they look up arrival and departure times for different flights.

They discuss their findings with customers and make reservations. Next, they calculate the cost for airline tickets and receive payments from customers. Finally, agents print out tickets and itineraries. In addition to planning trips for one or two people, agents also organize trips for large groups.

Agents often base recommendations on their own travel experiences. Thus, agents may visit hotels, resorts and restaurants to judge the comfort, cleanliness and quality of food and service. Travel agents also promote their own services.

They present slides or movies to social and special interest groups in order to find new customers. For customers who are just beginning to plan vacations, agents give them brochures about travel destinations.

Agents may advise international travellers about customs regulations, passports and visas and money exchange rates. In small offices, travel agents may type travel schedules, estimate costs and perform other clerical duties. In larger firms, office assistants perform these tasks.

Other titles and keywords for this career.

Work Activities: The following list of occupational tasks is specific to this career.

- Collect payment for transportation from customers.
- Ask customers about their travel plans in order to research travel options.
- Calculate rates for transportation and rooms.
- Reserve transportation and lodging for customers.
- Sell and plan group tours.
- Give customers brochures with information about things to do and see in various places.
- Print or request airline tickets, using computer.
- Visit hotels, resorts and restaurants. Give customers information about the places they have been.

People in this career perform the following list of tasks, but the tasks are common to many occupations.

- Work with the public.
- Get information needed to do the job.
- Convince others to buy goods or change their minds or actions.
- Use computers.
- Communicate with people from outside the organization.
- Update and use job-related knowledge.
- Establish and maintain relationships.
- Organize, plan and prioritize work.
- Communicate with supervisors, peers, or subordinates.

- Make decisions and solve problems.
- Document and record information.
- Explain the meaning of information to others.
- Resolve conflicts and negotiate with others.
- Perform administrative tasks.
- Judge the value of objects, services, or people.
- Process information.
- Think creatively.
- Analyze data or information.
- Assist others.
- Coordinate the activities of others.

Working Conditions: In a typical work setting, people in this career:

Interpersonal Relationships:

- Have a high level of social contact. They spend most of the day talking to customers.
- May sometimes deal with angry or unpleasant customers.
- Communicate with customers daily by telephone, e-mail, or in person.
- Are sometimes placed in conflict situations.
- Write letters and memos on a weekly basis.
- Work in a group or as part of a team.

Physical Work Conditions:

- Work indoors most of the time.
- Work somewhat close to other people, such as when sharing office space.

Work Performance:

- Must be highly exact in their work. Errors could cost customers money.
- Repeat the same tasks, such as answering phones and using computers.
- Must repeat the same activities.
- Often make decisions that affect customers. They consult supervisors for some decisions, but make most without talking to a supervisor.

- Are able to set some tasks for the day without consulting with a supervisor.
- Are highly competitive with other travel agents.
- Must meet strict deadlines on a weekly basis.

Hours/Travel:

- Generally have a set schedule each week.
- May work full time or part time, but most work 40 hours a week.
- May work more than 40 hours a week if self-employed.
- May work evenings and weekends, when people have time to plan vacations.

Physical Demands: People in this career frequently:

- Sit for long periods of time.

It is important for people in this career to be able to:

- Speak clearly so listeners can understand.
- Understand the speech of another person.
- See details of objects that are less than a few feet away.

It is not as important, but still necessary, for people in this career to be able to:

- Use fingers to grasp, move, or assemble very small objects.
- Focus on one source of sound and ignore others.
- Make fast, repeated movements of fingers, hands and wrists.
- See details of objects that are more than a few feet away.

Skills and Abilities: People in this career need to:

Communicate

- Listen to others, understand and ask questions.
- Express ideas clearly when speaking or writing.
- Read and understand written information.

Reason and Problem Solve:

- Notice when something is wrong or is likely to go wrong.
- Understand new information or materials by studying and working with them.

- Analyze ideas and use logic to determine their strengths and weaknesses.
- Concentrate and not be distracted while performing a task.
- Develop rules or follow guidelines for arranging items.
- Use reasoning to discover answers to problems.
- Judge the costs and benefits of a possible action.
- Think of new ideas or original and creative ways to solve problems.
- Identify problems and review information. Develop, review and apply solutions.
- Combine several pieces of information and draw conclusions.

Use Math and Science:

- Use math skills to solve problems.
- Add, subtract, multiply and divide quickly and correctly.

Manage Oneself, People, Time and Things:

- Manage the time of self and others.
- Check how well one is learning or doing something.
- Motivate, develop and direct people as they work.
- Go back and forth between two or more activities or sources of information without becoming confused.

Work with People:

- Look for ways to help people.
- Be aware of others¿ reactions and change behaviour in relation to them.
- Persuade others to approach things differently.
- Teach others how to do something, using several methods.

Knowledge: People in this career need knowledge in the following areas:

- *Customer and Personal Service:* Knowledge of providing special services to customers based on their needs.
- *Geography:* Knowledge of land, sea and air masses. Also includes knowledge of how to describe their location, features and relationships.

- *Sales and Marketing:* Knowledge of advertising and selling products and services.
- *Transportation:* Knowledge of ways to move people, goods, or materials. This may be by air, rail, sea, or road.
- *English Language:* Knowledge of the meaning, spelling and use of the English language.
- *Clerical:* Knowledge of general office work such as filing and recording information.
- *Computers and Electronics:* Knowledge of computer hardware and software.

Interests: People in this career are people who tend to:

- Consider relationships important. They like to work in a friendly, non-competitive environment. They like to do things for other people. They prefer jobs where they are not pressured to do things that go against their sense of right and wrong.
- Consider independence important. They like to make decisions and try out ideas on their own. They prefer jobs where they can plan their work with little supervision.
- Consider good working conditions important. They like jobs offering steady employment and good pay. They want employment that fits their individual work style. They may prefer doing a variety of tasks, working alone, or being busy all the time.
- Consider achievement important. They like to see the results of their work and to use their strongest abilities. They like to get a feeling of accomplishment from their work.
- Have enterprising interests. They like work activities that involve starting up and carrying out projects, especially in business. They like to lead and persuade others, make decisions and take risks for profit.
- Have social interests. They like work activities that assist others and promote learning and personal development. They like to communicate with others: to teach, give advice, help, or otherwise be of service to others.

- Have conventional interests. They like work activities that follow set procedures, routines and standards. They like to work with data and detail. They prefer working where there is a clear line of authority to follow.

Preparation: To work as a travel agent, you must:

complete a high school diploma or GED;

complete a travel agent training programme;

have excellent interpersonal skills; and

be self-motivated.

Formal Education: Travel agents must have at least a high school diploma or GED. Many have a bachelor's degree. Several majors are good preparation for this occupation. These include computers, geography, languages and history.

You also need to complete a travel agent course or programme. Many vocational schools offer programmes to train travel agents. These programmes last from six to 12 weeks. Completing a travel agent programme should help you get a job as a trainee. However, you should check the school's reputation with area employers before enrolling. Another option is the American Society of Travel Agents' correspondence course. This course provides a basic understanding of the travel industry.

Work Experience: A job as a reservation clerk or receptionist in a travel agency is good background for this occupation.

On-the-job Training: Once hired, new agents learn how to use their employers' computer systems. You may receive training for up to three months.

Outlook: In Minnesota, the number of jobs for travel agents is expected to decline through the year 2014. Nationally, the number of jobs for travel agents is expected to decline through the year 2014. Several factors are reducing the demand for travel agents. Travel agencies now have computerized reservation systems. These systems help agents find information more quickly and help more customers. In addition, customers can now make their own travel plans by using the Internet. These customers do not work with travel agents at all.

Also, airlines no longer pay commissions to travel agencies. This has reduced agencies' revenues and caused some to go out of business. However, some consumers still prefer to use a professional travel agent to ensure reliability, to save time and, in some cases, to save money.

The travel industry is sensitive to economic downturns because fewer people go on vacation during these periods. Therefore, the number of job opportunities for travel agents varies with the state of the economy.

Many job opportunities will arise as new agencies open and existing agencies expand. Most openings will occur as experienced agents leave this occupation.

	Employment	*Employment Change*		
	2002	2012	Number	Percent
National	102,700	96,400	-6,300	-6.1

Advancement Opportunities: Travel agents advance by gaining more clients and booking more trips. This usually results in higher wages. Some agents advance by specializing in one area of travel, such as cruises or group trips.

Tour Guides

Introduction: According to the World Tourism Organization, tourists are people who "travel to and stay in places outside their usual environment for not more than one consecutive year for leisure, business and other purposes not related to the exercise of an activity remunerated from within the place visited". Tourist Guide is the person who leads or directs the tourist through the latter's trip. With the recent boom in tourism, this sector offers excellent career prospects.

Eligibility

a. Age -No maximum age limit
b. Educational Qualifications -Preferably graduation degree in any discipline, preferably art, archeology, history and culture

Skills and Attributes: The tourism department holds examination depending on their needs and advertises it in leading newspapers. The test consists heavily of general knowledge, history and culture etc. For further details you can contact the regional offices of the tourism department.

The candidate should possess good linguistic skills especially verbal along with a pleasing personality. Knowledge of foreign language is an added advantage. IGNOU (Indira Gandhi National Open University), Indian Institute of Tourism and Travel Management, Gwalior with campuses at Delhi and Kurukshetra, Jammu University, Jammu, Bundelkhand University, Jhansi, Annamalai University, Chennai, Kurukshetra University, Kurukshetra are some of the institutes offering various courses in tourism management.

Recruitment Procedure: The candidates are selected generally on the basis of a written test. The pre-requisite for the test is a graduation degree in any discipline.

Job Prospects: This is a growing field which offers excellent opportunities in the field of tour operations, tour-packages, sight-seeing etc. Many employment opportunities exist in this industry. Travel services including tour operators, travel agents, hoteliers, restaurateurs transport service providers, adventure and leisure tourism providers, heritage sites and their conservation, manufacture and sale of handicraft items, marketing of souvenirs- all of which needs a degree of professionalism.

Besides the specialized services, there are the support services: administration in the offices, secretarial and clerical jobs. The Government of India has recognized the tourism sector as an industry thereby boosting the career.

Overview: Tour guides develop and oversee activities for groups of tourists or visitors.

Monument Valley, located along the Utah/Arizona border, is known as the ultimate desert landscape. Red sandstone cliffs jut up to 1,000 feet into the air. Even if you've never been there before, photos taken of Monument Valley might look familiar. This is because many old Westerns were filmed there.

You can drive through Monument Valley (which is a tribal park, part of the Navajo Nation) on select highways. However, visitors often say the best way to really view the scenery and understand its history is to go on a guided tour. Tour guides can take you on horseback or via jeeps into parts of the Valley not visible from the main road. They can also give you a bird's eye view of what it's like to live in Monument Valley, among the cliffs and mesas.

Some tour guides plan and oversee an entire vacation for a large group. They schedule activities for the group, such as sight seeing, outdoor sports and recreation and dining out. They also make time in the schedule for tourists to explore places on their own. Other tour guides are in charge of tours at a single site, such as a museum or around a city. They guide several different groups each day rather than travelling with one particular group.

Regardless of the type of tours they give, tour guides have many duties in common. First, they recruit people to give tours to. They talk to people and try to convince them to take the tour. They hand out brochures about their tour service and about the sites they will visit. They sell tickets and collect payments from those who want to take the tour. Depending on the tour, they may introduce clients to each other and hand out identification tags.

Tour guides are responsible for the groups of people they escort. They make sure no one gets lost or separated from the group. They also watch clients to make sure they follow tour rules. In museums, for example, guides make sure visitors do not touch the paintings. On the tour, they tell visitors about the sites they are seeing. They answer visitors' questions and recommend additional sites for them to see. Depending on the tour, guides may drive buses to transport clients around town or to new sites.

Tour guides have a few tasks specific to their employer. Those who travel with clients may carry clients' luggage to and from the bus. They may also collect and deliver mail and messages. Tour guides who work at sites such as museums may answer phones, type and file. They also monitor sites to make sure they are safe for visitors.

Tour guides often guide visitors from other countries. Thus, speaking a foreign language can be an advantage.

Other titles and keywords for this career.

Work Activities: The following list of occupational tasks is specific to this career.

- Conduct educational activities for school children.
- Escort groups on tours. Describe points of interest and background information.
- Answer questions about sites and recommend places to visit.
- Monitor visitors' behaviour when they are touring sites.
- Register members of group tours. Provide name tags and brochures.
- Monitor facilities to make sure they are safe and pleasant for tourists.
- Plan trips based on clients' skill and ability levels.
- Provide information about wildlife habitats and regulations.
- Distribute brochures and conduct presentations.
- Provide visitors with information and directions.
- Collect fees and tickets from group.
- Teach skills and proper use of equipment.
- Develop a schedule of activities for vacation tours.
- Sell tickets and souvenirs.
- Speak foreign languages to communicate with visitors from other countries.
- Prepare supplies and equipment before trip.
- Perform clerical duties such as typing, filing and collecting mail for vacationers.
- Drive vehicle to transport visitors to tour locations.
- Transport vacationers' luggage and travel bags.

People in this career perform the following list of tasks, but the tasks are common to many occupations.

- Work with the public.

- Get information needed to do the job.
- Establish and maintain relationships.
- Explain the meaning of information to others.
- Think creatively.
- Communicate with supervisors, peers, or subordinates.
- Identify objects, actions and events.
- Teach others.
- Update and use job-related knowledge.
- Communicate with people from outside the organization.
- Perform activities that use the whole body.
- Organize, plan and prioritize work.
- Make decisions and solve problems.
- Process information.

Working Conditions: In a typical work setting, people in this career:

Interpersonal Relationships

- Have a high level of job-required social interaction.
- Communicate with clients weekly in person.
- Must speak publicly on a weekly basis.
- Work in a group or as part of a team.

Physical Work Conditions:

- Work both indoors and outdoors, depending on the type of tour. Often work in indoor environments without heat or air conditioning.
- Work near other people, but usually have a few feet of space separating them from others.
- May wear a special uniform so clients can identify them easily.

Work Performance:

- Must be sure that a job is done accurately. Errors could mean clients do not get to visit all the sites on their schedule.
- Sometimes make decisions that affect their clients. They

consult supervisors for some decisions, but make most without talking to a supervisor.

- Are able to set some tasks for the day without talking to a supervisor.

Hours/Travel:

- Generally have a set schedule each week.
- May work part time or full time, but most work less than 40 hours a week.
- May work more during the summer when more people take vacations.

Physical Demands: People in this career frequently:

- Stand for long periods of time.

It is important for people in this career to be able to:

- Speak clearly so listeners can understand.
- Understand the speech of another person.

It is not as important, but still necessary, for people in this career to be able to:

- See details of objects whether they are nearby or far away.
- Use stomach and lower back muscles to support the body for long periods without getting tired.
- Be physically active for long periods without getting tired or out of breath.
- Use one or two hands to grasp, move, or assemble objects.
- Move two or more limbs together (for example, two arms, two legs, or one leg and one arm) while remaining in place.
- Coordinate movement of several parts of the body, such as arms and legs, while the body is moving.

Skills and Abilities: People in this career need to:

Communicate

- Express ideas clearly when speaking or writing.
- Listen to others, understand and ask questions.
- Read and understand work-related materials.

Reason and Problem Solve:

- Understand new information or materials by studying and working with them.
- Notice when something is wrong or is likely to go wrong.
- Analyze ideas and use logic to determine their strengths and weaknesses.
- Follow guidelines to arrange objects or actions in a certain order.
- Use reasoning to discover answers to problems.
- Combine several pieces of information and draw conclusions.

Manage Oneself, People, Time and Things:

- Check how well one is learning or doing something.
- Manage the time of self and others.

Work with People:

- Be aware of others¿ reactions and change behaviour in relation to them.
- Teach others how to do something, using several methods.
- Look for ways to help people.
- Persuade others to approach things differently.

Knowledge: People in this career need knowledge in the following areas:

- Customer and Personal Service: Knowledge of providing special services to customers based on their needs.
- History and Archeology: Knowledge of events that happened in the past. Also includes knowledge of the signs, causes and impact on people and cultures.
- English Language: Knowledge of the meaning, spelling and use of the English language.
- Public Safety and Security: Knowledge of protecting people, data and property.

Interests: People in this career are people who tend to:

- Consider relationships important. They like to work in a friendly, non-competitive environment. They like to do things for other people. They prefer jobs where they are

not pressured to do things that go against their sense of right and wrong.

- Have social interests. They like work activities that assist others and promote learning and personal development. They like to communicate with others: to teach, give advice, help, or otherwise be of service to others.
- Have enterprising interests. They like work activities that involve starting up and carrying out projects, especially in business. They like to lead and persuade others, make decisions and take risks for profit.

Preparation: To work as a tour guide, you must:

have a high school diploma or GED;

complete on-the-job training; and

have excellent interpersonal skills.

Formal Education: No formal education is required beyond high school. However, some tour guides learn skills through programmes offered by two-year colleges and travel associations. In this type of programme you study geography, history and communications. It is also helpful if you learn a language other than English. Training programmes last about nine months.

On-the-job Training: Many tour guides receive informal, on-the-job training from an employer or experienced worker. On the job, you learn:

customer service; and

site history or geography.

Training may last from a few months to a year.

Outlook: In Minnesota, the number of jobs for tour guides is expected to grow about as fast as average through the year 2014. Nationally, the number of jobs for tour guides is expected to grow as fast as average through the year 2014.

The need for tour guides may grow if the economy stays strong. The travel industry depends heavily on a good economy in which people have money to spend on travel. If the economy weakens, fewer people will travel. In addition, travellers may try to save money by following tour books instead of hiring tour guides.

	Employment	*Employment Change*		
	2002	2012	Number	Percent
National	38,000	44,200	6,200	16.3

Advancement Opportunities: Experienced tour guides with strong organizational skills may advance to managerial positions in tour companies. They may also set up their own tour businesses. Some tour guides become travel writers. Others get training and become travel agents.

Reservation and Ticket Agents

Overview: Reservation and ticket agents make and confirm reservations and sell travel tickets. In 2003, all the airlines in the US recorded 600 million passengers on their flights. That number is TWICE the population of the United States. This includes everyone from the business traveller who flies every week to the person who flew for the very first time. Nearly every single person had to reserve a seat on their particular flight. Usually, the person who handled that reservation was a reservation or ticket agent.

Most reservation agents work for airlines or large hotel chains. They help people plan trips and make reservations. They usually work in large reservation centres where they answer phone calls and offer travel ideas. Agents give information about travel routes, time schedules, rates and places to stay. They quote fares and room rates using computerized data. They also make and confirm travel schedules and hotel reservations.

Transportation ticket agents work in airports, train and bus stations. They sell tickets, assign seats to passengers and check baggage. In addition, they may answer questions, give directions, examine passports, or check in pets. Gate agents work in airports. They help passengers board airplanes. They direct passengers to boarding gates and check their tickets and seat assignments. Gate agents also make boarding announcements over public address systems. In addition, they help youth or passengers with disabilities to board the airplane.

Travel clerks usually work for member organizations such as auto clubs. They plan trips and offer travel suggestions such as the best route to take. They may also prepare an itinerary that shows points of interest, restaurants and motels.

Other titles and keywords for this career.

Work Activities: The following list of occupational tasks is specific to this career.

- Answer phone calls and offer suggestions on travel arrangements.
- Quote fares and room rates and provide travel information.
- Make and confirm transportation and hotel reservations, using a computer.
- Sell and issue tickets, assign seats and check baggage.
- May answer questions, give directions and check passports.
- Direct passengers to boarding areas and check tickets and seat assignments.
- Make boarding announcements.
- Assist children or passengers with disabilities when they board.

People in this career perform the following list of tasks, but the tasks are common to many occupations.

- Use computers.
- Work with the public.
- Resolve conflicts and negotiate with others.
- Document and record information.
- Establish and maintain relationships.
- Communicate with people from outside the organization.
- Process information.
- Make decisions and solve problems.
- Get information needed to do the job.
- Explain the meaning of information to others.
- Communicate with supervisors, peers, or subordinates.
- Convince others to buy goods or change their minds or actions.
- Organize, plan and prioritize work.

- Evaluate information against standards.
- Assist others.
- Update and use job-related knowledge.
- Identify objects, actions and events.
- Coordinate the work and activities of others.
- Develop and build teams.
- Coach others.

Working Conditions: In a typical work setting, people in this career:

Interpersonal Relationships:

- Have a high level of social contact. They work closely with passengers and customers.
- Communicate a great deal by telephone and in person. They also write letters, memos and e-mail, but less frequently.
- Sometimes are placed in conflict situations in which passengers may become unpleasant or angry.
- May work as part of a team.

Physical Work Conditions:

- Often work indoors, but may on rare occasions work outdoors.
- Often wear a company uniform.
- Are often exposed to loud sounds and distracting noise levels, such as from departing and arriving planes.
- Often share workspace with other ticket agents.

Work Performance:

- Repeat the same physical and mental tasks.
- Must be sure that all details are done and their work is exact. Errors could disrupt passengers' travel plans.
- Must keep pace with the speed of computers and ticketing equipment.
- Must meet strict daily and weekly deadlines.

Hours/Travel:

- May work part time or full time. Schedules are usually established.

- May be required to work evenings, late night shifts, weekends and holidays.

Physical Demands: People in this career frequently:

- Sit when assisting passengers and answering telephone calls.
- Repeat movements over and over.
- Use hands to handle, control, or feel objects or controls.

It is important for people in this career to be able to:

- See details of objects that are less than a few feet away.
- Speak clearly so listeners can understand.

It is not as important, but still necessary, for people in this career to be able to:

- Make fast, repeated movements of fingers, hands and wrists.
- Focus on one source of sound and ignore others.
- Understand the speech of another person.
- Use stomach and lower back muscles to support the body for long periods without getting tired.

Skills and Abilities: People in this career need to:

Communicate

- Listen to others, understand and ask questions.
- Express ideas clearly when speaking.
- Read and understand written information.

Reason and Problem Solve:

- Analyze ideas and use logic to determine their strengths and weaknesses.
- Understand new information or materials by studying and working with them.
- Judge the costs and benefits of a possible action.
- Remember information such as words, numbers, pictures and procedures.
- Concentrate and not be distracted while performing a task.
- Follow guidelines to arrange objects or actions in a certain order.

- Identify problems and review information. Develop, review and apply solutions.

Use Math and Science:

- Add, subtract, multiply and divide quickly and correctly.

Manage Oneself, People, Time and Things:

- Manage the time of self and others.
- Check how well one is learning or doing something.

Work with People:

- Look for ways to help people.
- Use several methods to learn or teach others how to do something.
- Be aware of others¿ reactions and change behaviour in relation to them.
- Persuade others to approach things differently.

Work with Things:

- Operate and control equipment.

Knowledge: People in this career need knowledge in the following areas:

- Customer and Personal Service: Knowledge of providing special services to customers based on their needs.
- English Language: Knowledge of the meaning, spelling and use of the English language.
- Public Safety and Security: Knowledge of protecting people, data and property.
- Transportation: Knowledge of ways to move people, goods, or materials. This may be by air, rail, sea, or road.

Interests: People in this career are people who tend to:

- Consider support from their employer important. They like to be treated fairly and have supervisors who will back them up. They prefer jobs where they are trained well.
- Consider relationships important. They like to work in a friendly, non-competitive environment. They like to do things for other people. They prefer jobs where they are

not pressured to do things that go against their sense of right and wrong.

- Consider good working conditions important. They like jobs offering steady employment and good pay. They want employment that fits their individual work style. They may prefer doing a variety of tasks, working alone, or being busy all the time.
- Have conventional interests. They like work activities that follow set procedures, routines and standards. They like to work with data and detail. They prefer working where there is a clear line of authority to follow.
- Have enterprising interests. They like work activities that involve starting up and carrying out projects, especially in business. They like to lead and persuade others, make decisions and take risks for profit.
- Have social interests. They like work activities that assist others and promote learning and personal development. They like to communicate with others: to teach, give advice, help, or otherwise be of service to others.

Preparation: To work as a reservation and ticket agent, you must:

have a high school diploma or GED; and

complete on-the-job training.

On-the-job Training: Most airline reservation and ticket agents learn their skills through company training programmes. In a classroom setting, you learn company policies and ticketing procedures. You learn to use the airline's computer system to get information and make reservations. You also learn about airline regulations and safety procedures. After training, a supervisor or experienced agent monitors your work for a period.

In contrast, auto clubs, bus lines and railroads tend to train their ticket agents and travel clerks on the job. They provide short, in-house classes that last a few days.

Military Training: The military is a good source of training for this occupation.

Outlook: In Minnesota, the outlook for this occupation is currently not available.

Nationally, the number of jobs for reservation and ticket agents is expected to show little or no change through the year 2014. A growing population is expected to demand more travel services. However, growth in this occupation will be slowed by technological advances. By using computers, agents can make more reservations and issue more tickets in less time. In addition, many passengers check fares and make reservations on the Internet. Nevertheless, job openings will continue to occur as agents retire or transfer to other occupations.

Competition will be strong for jobs as reservation and ticket agents. Entry requirements are few and many people seeking to enter the travel business start in these types of jobs. Also, people are attracted to this occupation because it provides excellent travel benefits. However, the travel industry is affected by the state of the economy. When the economy is slow, people travel less. As a result, employers are less likely to hire new workers and may even lay people off.

	Employment	*Employment Change*		
	2002	2012	Number	Percent
National	163,000	166,800	3,800	2.3

Advancement Opportunities: Reservation and ticket agent jobs offer good opportunities to get started in the airline or travel business. In the airline industry, workers are often promoted through the ranks. For example, an experienced ticket agent may advance to lead worker on the shift. Agents who obtain additional skills, experience and training improve their chances for advancement. A college degree may be required for advancement to management.

Travel Clerks

Significant Points: Most jobs are found in large metropolitan airports, downtown ticket offices, large reservation centres and train or bus stations.

A high school diploma or its equivalent is the most common educational requirement.

Employment is expected to grow more slowly than average because of the significant impact of technology on worker productivity. Applicants for jobs are likely to encounter considerable competition; those who have previous experience in the travel industry, in sales, or in customer service should have the best chances.

Nature of the Work: Each year, millions of Americans travel by plane, train, ship, bus and automobile. Many of these travellers rely on the services of reservation and transportation ticket agents and travel clerks, who perform functions as varied as selling tickets, confirming reservations, checking baggage and providing tourists with useful travel information.

Most *reservation agents* work for large hotel chains or airlines, helping people to plan trips and make reservations. They usually work in large reservation centres, answering telephone or e-mail inquiries and offering suggestions and information about travel arrangements, such as routes, schedules, rates and types of accommodation. Reservation agents quote fares and room rates, provide travel information and make and confirm transportation and hotel reservations. Most agents use proprietary networks to obtain, as quickly as possible, information needed to make, change, or cancel reservations for customers.

Transportation ticket agents are sometimes known as passenger service agents, passenger booking clerks, reservation clerks, airport service agents, ticket clerks, or ticket sellers. They work in airports, train stations and bus stations, selling tickets, assigning seats to passengers and checking baggage. In addition, they may answer inquiries and give directions, examine passports and visas, or check in pets.

They may be required assist customers who have trouble operating self-service ticket printing machines, which also are known as kiosks. Other ticket agents, more commonly known as *gate* or *station agents*, work in airport terminals, assisting passengers boarding airplanes. These workers direct passengers to the correct boarding area, check tickets and seat assignments, make boarding announcements and provide special assistance to young, elderly, or disabled passengers when they board or disembark.

Most *travel clerks* are employed by membership organizations, such as automobile clubs. These workers, sometimes called *member services counsellors* or *travel counsellors*, plan trips, calculate mileage and offer travel suggestions, such as the best route from the point of origin to the destination, to club members. Travel clerks also may prepare an itinerary indicating points of interest, restaurants, overnight accommodations and availability of emergency services during a trip. In some cases, they make rental car, hotel and restaurant reservations for club members.

Passenger rate clerks generally work for bus companies. They sell tickets for regular bus routes and arrange non-scheduled or chartered trips. They plan travel routes, compute rates and keep customers informed of appropriate details. They also may arrange travel accommodations.

Working Conditions: Most reservation and transportation ticket agents and travel clerks work in areas that are clean and well lit. This is especially true for agents who greet customers and visitors in person. Reservation and ticket agents may spend much of their day talking on the telephone; however, they commonly work away from the public, often in large centralized reservation or phone centres. Because a large number of agents or clerks may share the same workspace, it may be crowded and noisy.

Although most reservation and transportation ticket agents and travel clerks work a standard 40-hour week, about 2 out of 10 work part time. Some high school and college students are employed part time in this occupation, working after school or during vacations. Some agents work evenings, late nights, weekends and holidays. In general, employees with the most seniority tend to be assigned the more desirable shifts.

The work performed by reservation and transportation ticket agents and travel clerks may be repetitive and stressful. They often work under stringent time constraints or must meet quotas on the number of calls answered or reservations made. Difficult or angry customers also can create stressful situations as agents usually bear the brunt of customers' dissatisfaction. Agents may work on their feet for a large portion of their shift and may have to lift heavy baggage. In addition, prolonged exposure to a computer monitor, which is common in this occupation, may lead to eyestrain.

Training, Other Qualifications and Advancement: A high school diploma or its equivalent is the most common educational requirement for reservation and transportation ticket agent and travel clerk jobs. Some employers, however, prefer applicants who have completed college coursework in management or business. Experience with computers, including good typing skills, also is usually required. Some jobs require applicants to be over 18 years of age and posses a valid driver's license. Agents who handle passenger luggage must be able to lift heavy objects.

Most airline reservation and ticket agents learn their skills through formal company training programmes that can last several weeks. Here, they learn company and industry policies as well as ticketing procedures. Trainees also learn to use the airline's computer system to obtain information on schedules, fares and the availability of seats; to make reservations for passengers; and to plan passenger itineraries. In addition, they must become familiar with airport and airline code designations, regulations and safety procedures. After completing classroom instruction, new agents work under the direct guidance of a supervisor or experienced agent. During this time the supervisors may, for example, monitor telephone conversations to improve the quality of customer service so that agents learn to provide customer service in a courteous manner, while limiting the time spent on each call.

In contrast to those who work for airlines, reservation and transportation ticket agents and travel clerks who work for automobile clubs, bus lines and railroads are trained on the job through short in-house classes that last several days.

Many reservation and transportation ticket agents and travel clerks deal directly with the public, so a professional appearance and a pleasant personality are important. A clear speaking voice and fluency in the English language also are essential, because these employees frequently use the telephone or public-address systems. In addition, fluency in a foreign language is becoming increasingly helpful for those seeking reservation and ticket agent jobs.

Reservation and transportation ticket agents and travel clerks may advance by being transferred to a position with more responsibilities, or by being promoted to a supervisory position. Many travel companies fill supervisory and managerial positions by promoting individuals within their organization, so those who acquire additional skills, experience and training improve their opportunities for advancement. Some companies require that candidates for supervisory positions have an associate degree in a business-related field, such as management, business administration, or marketing. Within the airline industry, a ticket agent may advance to lead worker on the shift.

Employment: Reservation and transportation ticket agents and travel clerks held about 163,000 jobs in 2004. About 6 out of 10 are employed by airlines. Others work for automobile clubs, hotels and other lodging places, railroad companies, bus lines and other companies that provide transportation services.

Although agents and clerks are found throughout the country, most work in large metropolitan airports, downtown ticket offices, large reservation centres and train or bus stations. The remainder work in small, regional airports, or in small communities served only by intercity bus or railroad lines.

Job Outlook: Applicants for reservation and transportation ticket agent jobs are likely to encounter considerable competition, because the supply of qualified applicants will exceed the expected number of job openings. Entry requirements for these jobs are minimal and many people seeking to get into the airline industry or another travel-related business often start out in such positions. The jobs provide excellent travel benefits and many people view airline and other travel-related jobs as glamorous. Applicants who have previous experience in the travel industry, in sales, or in customer service should have the best chances.

Employment of reservation and transportation ticket agents and travel clerks is expected to grow more slowly than the average for all occupations through 2014. Although a growing population will demand additional travel services, employment of these workers will grow more slowly than this demand because of the significant impact of technology on worker productivity. Automated reservations and ticketing, as well as "ticketless" travel, for example, are reducing the need for some workers. Most train stations and airports now have self-service ticket printing machines, called kiosks, which enable passengers to make reservations, purchase tickets and check-in for train rides and flights themselves.

Many passengers also are able to check flight times and fares, make reservations, purchase tickets and check-in for flights on the Internet. Nevertheless, not all travel-related passenger services can be fully automated, primarily for safety and security reasons. As a result, job openings will continue to become available as the occupation grows and as workers transfer to other occupations, retire, or leave the labour force altogether. Employment of reservation and transportation ticket agents and travel clerks is sensitive to cyclical swings in the economy. During recessions, discretionary passenger travel and transportation service companies are less likely to hire new workers and may even resort to layoffs.

Earnings: Median annual earnings of reservation and transportation ticket agents and travel clerks in May 2004 were $27,750. The middle 50 percent earned between $21,430 and $39,410. The lowest 10 percent earned less than $17,720 and the highest 10 percent earned more than $45,100. Many employers offer discounts on travel services to their employees. In May 2004, median annual earnings in the industries employing the larges number of agents were:

Scheduled air transportation	$31,750
Travel arrangement and reservation services	22,370
Traveller accommodation	22,050

Tourism Officer

Public Sector: The public sector offers a number of opportunities for graduates of tourism specifically in the areas of information provision and tourism management and development. Graduates of tourism from WIT with several years of experience would ultimately aspire to the following senior positions:

The Tourism Officer: From an administrative point of view Ireland is split up into a number of tourist regions each of these being managed through a Regional Tourism Authority (RTA). Most RTAs have several tourism officers to whom responsibility is given to develop and promote tourism in a particular geographic area. The main role of tourism officers in Ireland is the marketing and the development of tourism services and facilities. Tourism Officers and Senior Tourism Officers usually work closely with the residents and businesses of a local community and have a very important role in tourism development and maximising economic benefit for that community.

Typical work activities include:

- Strategic tourism planning and development;
- Providing advice to local businesses;
- Conducting research;
- Devising and managing marketing and promotional campaigns;
- Writing and screening funding applications;
- Managing staff and budgets;

Tourist Information Office Managers: Ireland has a network of Tourist Information Offices (TIO) all over the country providing tourist information and reservation facilities to the public on tourist attractions & facilities, accommodation and transportation. Managers are responsible for the day-to-day running of the TIO. This is a dynamic and rewarding area of work but at the same time it is very demanding and can involve long hours for relatively low pay. Typically day to day activities would include:

- Recruiting, training and motivating of staff; -Providing information to the public; -Generating business for member organisations;
- Administrative duties such as compiling reports & statistics and budgeting etc.;

- Selling merchandise;
- Assisting the tourism officer in researching and marketing local amenities.

Entertaining your Community

Introduction: The task of tourism officers is to attract business visitors and tourists to their area, balancing financial benefits against the needs of residents and the environment. They are employed in most councils–especially those in areas of natural beauty or historical significance/interest and of course near the sea. However, in recent years other local authorities in non-traditional tourist areas have seen the benefit of promoting their areas to attract tourists. Tourism is a fast growing and important aspect of many councils' work.

Work Environment: Tourism officers spend most of their time in offices within the local authority. Some travel between different locations within the area is required to attend meetings, give presentations, and staff promotional events etc. They may, on occasions, work unsociable hours.

Daily Activities: A major industry, tourism can have an enormous impact on a town or region. Local heritage and landscape can attract business and other visitors, bringing revenue throughout the year. An increasing number of authorities have appointed tourism officers to develop this potential. The work is varied and involves:

- promoting existing attractions; working with press and public relations people, designers and photographers to advertise local features. Where there is little history of tourism, the job also involves research into local history and developing potential attractions;
- engineering newsworthy events in order to generate publicity in the local, national and trade media;
- organising exhibition stands at conferences and at exhibitions both nationally and overseas to promote the area;

Bibliography

Albarran, Alan B. and Gregory G. Pitts: *The Radio Broadcasting Industry*, Boston, Allyn and Bacon, 2001.

Albrecht, Ulrich: *A Short Research Guide on Arms and Armed Forces*, New York, Facts on File, 1980.

Alexander, James: *Internships in Communications, Ames*, Iowa State University Press, 1995.

Allman, Paul: *Careers in Video and Digital Video*, New York: Rosen, 2001.

Anders, Peter: *Envisioning Cyberspace*, New York, McGraw-Hill, 1999.

Arkin, William M.: *Research Guide to Current Military and Strategic Affairs*, Washington, Institute for Policy Studies, 1981.

Baehr, H. and Gary A.: *Turning In On: A Reader in Women and Media*, London, Arnold, 1996.

Ball, Victoria Kloss: *Opportunities in Interior Design and Decorating Careers*, Chicago, VGM Career Horizons, 2002.

Barnouw, Erik: *A Tower in Babel: the History of Broadcasting in the United States to 1933*, New York, Oxford University Press, 1966.

Baucom, Alfred H.: *Hospitality Design for the Graying Generation: Meeting the Needs of a Growing Market*, New York, Wiley, 1996.

Baxter, John: *Australian Cinema*, Sydney, Pacific Books, 1970.

Beaman, Jim: *Interviewing for Radio*, New York, Routledge, 2000.

Berkowitz, Ira: *Vault Career Guide to Advertising*, New York, Vault, 2004.

Bertrand, Ina and Diane Collins: *Government and Film in Australia*, Sydney, Currency Press, 1981.

Bliss, Edward and James L. Hoyt: *Writing News for Broadcast*, New York, Columbia University Press, 1994.

Boella, Michael John: *Principles of Hospitality Law*, London, Cassell, 1999.

Bone, Jan, & Ana Fernandez: *Opportunities in Film Careers*, New York, VGM Career Books, 2004.

Bowers, C. A.: *The Cultural Dimension of Educational Computing: Understanding the Non-neutrality of Technology*, New York, Teachers' College Press; 1988.

Boyd, Andrew: *Broadcast Journalism: Techniques of Radio and TV News*, Woburn, Focal Press, 2001.

Brown, Douglas Robert: *The Restaurant Managers Handbook: How to Set Up, Operate, and Manage a Financially Successful Restaurant*. Lauderhill, Atlantic Pub., 1991.

Brown, James and Quaal Ward: *Radio-Television-Cable Management*, New York, McGraw Hill, 1998.

Bryant, Jennings: *Television and the American Family*, Hillsdale, Lawrence Erlbaum, 1990.

Buckingham, David: *Young People and the Media*, New York, Manchester University Press, 1993.

Buckner, Robert W.: *Site Selection: New Advancements in Methods and Technology*, New York, Lebhar-Friedman Books, 1998.

Caldwell, J. T.: *Electronic Media and Technoculture*, New Brusnwick, Rutgers University Press, 2000.

Careers in Focus: *Photography*, New York, Ferguson, 2004.

Carmouche, Rita: *Behavioural Studies in Hospitality Management*, New York, Chapman & Hall, 1995.

Carroll, Victoria: *Writing News for Television*, Ames, Iowa State University Press, 1997.

Cassiday, Doris, and Bruce Cassiday: *Careers in the Beauty Industry*, New York, Franklin Watts, 1978.

Clark, Mona: *Interpersonal Skills for Hospitality Managers*, London, Chapman Hill, 1995.

Clark, Roy Peter: *A Journalist Teaches Young Writers*, Portsmouth, Heinemann, 1987.

Cockburn, C. and Ormrod, S.: *Gender and Technology in the Making*, London, Sage, 1993.

Cohler, David Keith: *Broadcast Newswriting*, Englewood Cliffs, Prentice Hall, 1990.

Cracknell, H. L.: *Escoffier: The Complete Guide to the Art of Modern Cookery*, New York, John Wiley, 1979.

Craig, James: *Graphic Design Career Guide*, New York, Watson-Guptill, 1992.

Crawford, Tad: *Starting Your Career As a Freelance Photographer*, New York, Allworth Press, 2003.

Crouse, Chuck: *Reporting for Radio*, Chicago, Bonus Books, 1998.

Davidson, M. J. and Cooper, C. L.: *Women and Information Technology*, New York, John Wiley & Sons, 1987.

Delaney, Chuck: *Photography Your Way*, New York, Allworth Press, 2005.

Dennis, Everette E. and Edward C. Pease: *Children and the Media*, New Brunswick, Transaction Publishers, 1996.

Diamond, S. Taylor's Way: *Women, Cultures and Technology*, New York: Routledge; 1997.

Donald, Ralph and Thomas Spann: *Fundamentals of Television Production*, Ames, Iowa State University Press, 2000.

Dornenburg, Andrew: *Culinary Artistry*, New York, John Wiley & Sons, 1996.

Douglas, George H.: *The Early Days of Radio Broadcasting*, Jefferson, NC: McFarland, 1987.

Easlea, B.: *Fathering the Unthinkable: Masculinity, Scientists and the Nuclear Arms Race*, London, Pluto Press, 1982.

Ellis, Elmo: *Opportunities in Broadcasting Careers*, Chicago, VGM Career Books, 2005.

Faulkner, W. and Arnold, E.: *Smothered by Invention: Technology in Women's Lives*, London, Pluto Press, 1985.

Fensch, Thomas: *Television News Anchors*, Jefferson, McFarland, 1993.

Field, Shelly: *Career Opportunities in Advertising and Public Relations*, New York, Ferguson, 2006.

Foster, Timothy R. V.: *How to Succeed As an Independent Consultant*, London: Kogan, Page, 2002.

Fox Keller, E.: *Reflections on Gender and Science*, New Haven, Yale University Press, 1985.

Gardner, Garth: *Careers in Computer Graphics and Animation*, Fairfax, GGC, 2001.

Gibbs, Jenny: *Interior Design*, New York, H. N. Abrams, 2005.

Go, Frank M.: *Human Resource Management in the Hospitality Industry*, New York, Wiley, 1996.

Goldfarb, Roz: *Careers by Design*, New York, Allworth Press, 2001.

Gordon, Sandra R.: *Great Jobs for Film Majors*, Chicago, VGM Career Books, 2004.

Graham, Duane: *The Remarkable Story of Otto Graham*, Wayne, Immortal Investments Publishing, 2004.

Green, E. and Adam, A. Virtual Gender: *Technology, Consumption, and Identity*, New York, Routledge, 2001.

Greenman, Robert: *The Adviser's Companion*, New York, Columbia Scholastic Press Association, 1991.

Griffiths, D.: *The Exclusion of Women from Technology*, London, Pluto Press, 1985.

Hall, Ken G.: *Australian Film: the Inside Story*, Sydney, Summit Books, 1980.

Hewitt, John: *Airwords: Writing for Broadcast News, Mountain View*, Oxford, Mayfield Pub. Company, 2002.

Higham, Robin: *A Guide to the Sources of United States Military History*, Hamden, Archon Books, 1975.

Hilliard, Robert L. and Michael C. Keith: *The Broadcast Century and Beyond*, Boston: Focal Press, 2001.

Hinkin, Timothy R.: *Cases in Hospitality Management: A Critical Incident Approach*, New York, Wiley, 1995.

Holloway, J. C. : *Towards a Core Curriculum for Tourism: A Discussion Paper*, London, The National Liaison Group for Higher Education in Tourism, 1995.

Horstede, G.: *Cultures and Organizations: Software of the Mind*, London, McGraw-Hill Book Company, 1991.

Hungerland, Buff: *Marketing Your Creative Portfolio*, Upper Saddle River, Prentice Hall, 2003

Jain, S. C.: *Women and Technology*, Jaipur, Rawat Publications, 1985.

Jefferson, Michael: *Breaking into Graphic Design*, New York, Allworth Press, 2005.

Jensen, Clayne R.: *Opportunities in Recreation and Leisure Careers*, Lincolnwood, VGM Career Horizons, 2000.

Jones, Sue Jenklyn: *Fashion Design*, New York, Watson-Guptill, 2002.

Kieffer, John: *The Photographer's Assistant*, New York, Allworth, 2001.

Kirkham, P.: *The Gendered Object*, Manchester, Manchester University Press, 1996.

Kissane, Sharon F.: *Career Success for People with Physical Disabilities*, Lincolnwood, VGM Career Horizons, 1997.

Kring, Robin: *Party Creations: Book of Theme Event Design*, Denver, Clear Creek Pub., 1993.

Kurzweil, R.: *The Age of Spiritual Machines*, New York, Viking, 1999.

Lavery, P.: *Tourism Marketing and Management Handbook*, New York, Prentice Hall, 1989.

Lewis, Robert C.: *Cases in Hospitality Marketing and Management*, New York, John Wiley, 1997.

MacCloskey, Monro: *How to Qualify for the Service Academies*, New York, Richards Rosen Press, 1964.

Maclay, Edgar Stanton: *A History of the United States Navy 1771-1893*, New York, Appleton Co., 1894.

Mauro, Lucia: *Careers for Fashion Plates and Other Trendsetters*, Chicago, VGM Career Horizons, 2003.

McGuire-Lytle, Erin: *Careers in Graphic Arts and Computer Graphics*, New York, Rosen, 1999.

Miller, Samuel D.: *An Aerospace Bibliography*, Washington. Office of Air Force History, 1978.

Mitchell, Leslie Scott: *Freelancing for Television and Radio*, London; Routledge, 2005.

Mogel, Leonard: *Creating Your Career in Communications and Entertainment*, Sewickley, GATF Press, 1998.

Noronha, Shonan F. R.: *Opportunities in Television and Video Careers*, Chicago: VGM Career Books, 2003.

Orlik, Peter B.: *Career Perspectives in Electronic Media*, Ames, Blackwell Pub., 2004.

Packard, Sidney: *The Fashion Business: Dynamics and Careers*, New York, Holt, Rinehart, and Winston, 1983.

Parks, Peggy J.: *The News Media*, San Diego, Lucent Books, 2002.

Paullin, C.O.: *The Navy of the American Revolution*, Cleveland, The Burrows Brothers Co., 1906.

Perna, Rita: *Fashion Forecasting*, New York, Fairchild Publications, 1987.

Rachlis, Eugene: *The Story of the U.S. Coast Guard*, New York, Random House, 1961.

Reis, Ronald A.: *Careers in Art and Graphic Design*, Hauppage, Barrons, 2001.

Rocha, Tony L.: *Careers in Magazine Publishing*, New York, Rosen, 2001.

Rubinstein, Donna: *The Modeling Life*, New York, Berkeley Publishing Group, 1998.

Satterthwaite, Frank: *The Career Portfolio Workbook*, New York, McGraw-Hill, 2003.

Seguin, James: *Media Career Guide*, Boston, St. Martin's, 2006.

Sones, Melissa: *Getting into Fashion: A Career Guide*, New York, Ballantine, 1984.

Vogt, Peter: *Career Opportunities in the Fashion Industry*, New York, Facts on File, 2002.

Wilson, Wayne: *Careers in Publishing and Communications*, Bear, Mitchell Lane, 2002.

Yager, Fred, & Jan Yager: *Career Opportunities in the Film Industry*, New York, Ferguson, 2003.

Zahler, Karen Gantz.: *Superchefs: Signature Recipes From America's New Royalty*, New York, John Wiley & Sons, 1996.

Index

D

E

F

G

H

I